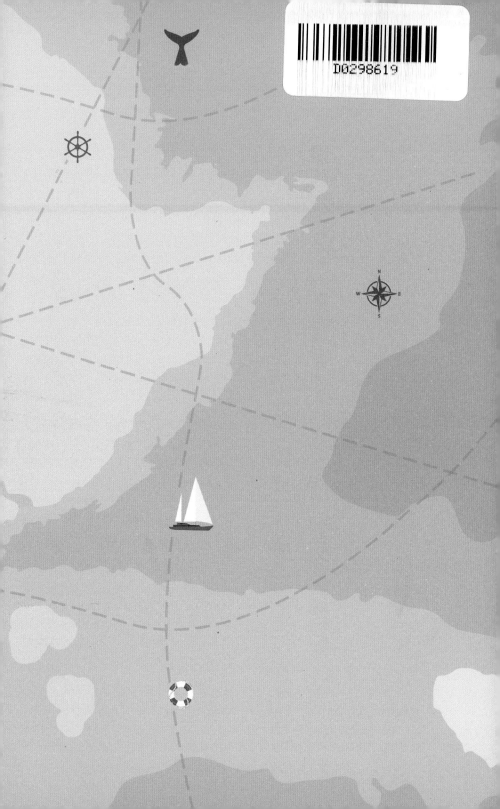

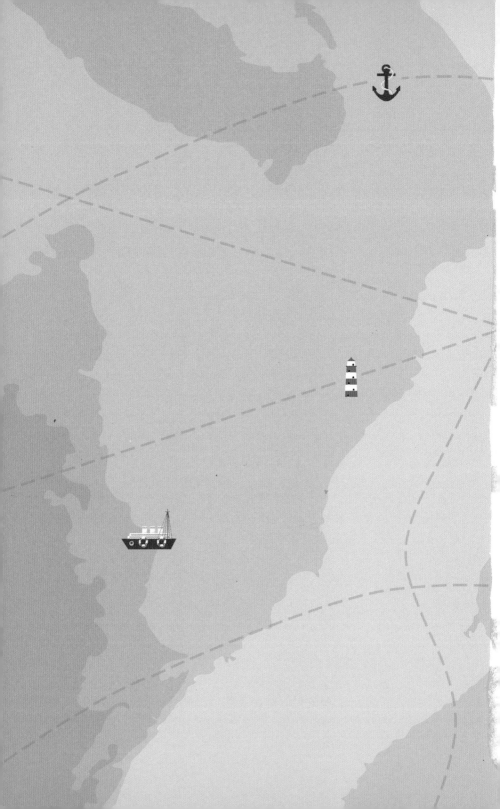

THE NAUTICAL PUZZLE BOOK

THE NAUTICAL PUZZLE BOOK

THE NATIONAL MARITIME MUSEUM

PUZZLES BY

DR. GARETH MOORE

HODDER &
STOUGHTON

First published in Great Britain in 2020 by Hodder & Stoughton
An Hachette UK company

1

Copyright © National Maritime Museum 2020

Page 24-25 © iStock
Page 26-27, 29, 81 © Shutterstock
Page 81© Getty Images
Page 149 © DeAgostini/Getty Images
Page 262 © Cambridge University Library
All other images © National Maritime Museum

A CIP catalogue record for this title is available from the British Library

Hardback ISBN 9781529322811
eBook ISBN 9781529322828

Gareth would like to thank his assistants Laura Jayne Ayres and Elizabeth
Crowdy for their help in researching and creating the puzzles for this book.

Designed and typeset by Craig Burgess

Reproduction by Alta London UK

Printed and bound in China by C&C Offset Ltd

Hodder & Stoughton policy is to use papers that are natural, renewable
and recyclable products and made from wood grown in sustainable forests.
The logging and manufacturing processes are expected to conform to the
environmental regulations of the country of origin.

Hodder & Stoughton Ltd
Carmelite House
50 Victoria Embankment
London EC4Y 0DZ

www.rmg.co.uk
www.hodder.co.uk

CONTENTS

INTRODUCTION

The ocean has always been a source of epic stories of endeavour and exploration. Our relationship with the sea – through work, play, love, loss, hope and despair – helps shape human identity, making us who we are, as individuals and societies. You can discover these epic stories of adventure at the National Maritime Museum, in Greenwich, London – the world's largest and most-visited museum of seafaring. Its vast collection has provided the inspiration for this book of puzzles, which will take you on a voyage around the globe.

A BRIEF HISTORY OF THE NATIONAL MARITIME MUSEUM

The National Maritime Museum was opened by King George VI on 27 April 1937 and was the result of ten years' preparatory work. This began in 1927, when James Caird (1864–1954), a Scottish shipowner and member of the Society for Nautical Research, bought a collection of maritime prints, drawings and paintings from Arthur Macpherson, a passionate sailor and voracious collector, on the understanding it would become the core of a new 'national naval and nautical museum'. And so, the National Maritime Museum was born.

Since then the museum has continued to grow and develop, modernising its facilities and improving its displays to meet public demand. The galleries and collections allow visitors to discover ships and boats of all shapes and sizes, and to voyage across the world's oceans. The museum holds over 2.6 million items in the collection, and its displays showcase this vast wealth of material.

The collection includes:

- 90,000 sea charts
- 4,000 oil paintings
- 70,000 prints and drawings
- 1 million ship plans
- up to 1 million historic photographs
- 44,500 3D objects, including small craft, ship models, coins and medals, decorative art, figureheads, relics, scientific instruments, uniforms and weapons
- 12 km of shelving for books and manuscripts

This book contains over 100 puzzles, many of which have been inspired by the museum's objects and their stories, including maps, ships, nautical terminology, explorers, myths, legends, iconography and seafaring traditions. The puzzles will test your general knowledge, observation and interpretation skills along the way. Travel through the book in any order you like – there's no set route on this voyage! Some may be more challenging, but you can always keep going and turn back and rediscover what you missed.

By the time you reach the end you'll have navigated centuries of history, crossed thousands of miles of ocean, and made countless discoveries – so batten down the hatches and set sail!

CHAPTER 1

SIGNS OF THE SEA

Maritime history is rich with symbolism. From flags, ship names, ships' badges, maritime tattoos and Royal Navy ranks, there is a wealth of meaning in each and every one. These signs of the sea are the focus of this chapter. Some may be familiar to you, others less so, but don't let that stop you – use the following word puzzles, general knowledge and multiple-choice questions to unpick a wealth of nautical iconography.

ANCHOR NAMES

There are many different types of anchor, all with their own characteristics. By deleting one letter from each pair of letters given below, can you reveal the names of the six pictured anchors? For example, CD AB OT would be concealing CAT.

1.   AS TL PO NE SE   TA VN OD   NR OU RP EM

2.   HP OR GI ML EI TS GI VO TE

3.   LE TA DS OT   IR SN ED AI AP TN

4.   MA ED EM IB RP HA LS NT YR

5.   RP LA TO MU NG HS

6.   AP HO RO ST EF RE

Bonus Question:

What is the name given to the iconic maritime symbol of an anchor with coiled ropes or chains around it? As a clue, it is also a description of any real anchor with ropes or cables tangled around it.

1.

2.

3.

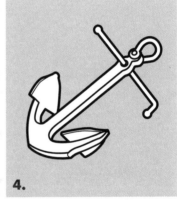

4.

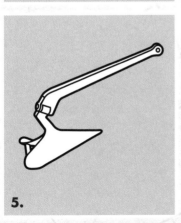

5.

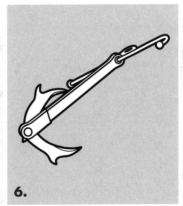

6.

ANCHOR PARTS

This picture shows the names of the different parts of an anchor. Based on this, can you match the descriptions of each anchor below to the correct picture?

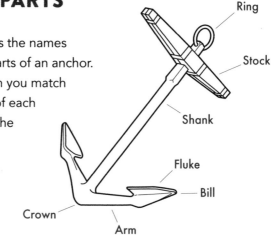

Ring

Stock

Shank

Fluke

Bill

Crown

Arm

1. STOCKLESS

- No stock
- Two arms are parallel and point in the same direction
- The arms curve to a pointed bill

2. WISHBONE

- The shank is split into two parts and joined at the top, resembling a wishbone
- One straight arm to which the shank and flukes are attached

3. MUSHROOM

- Curved, circular base attaching to the shank
- No stock

4. NORTHILL

- The two arms have flukes and pointed bills, resembling ploughs
- The stock passes through the crown

5. DANFORTH

- The stock is located at the crown
- Two flat flukes attach to the stock and point in the same direction

6. CHINESE

- Two straight arms angled upwards in a 'V' shape
- The stock, with three component parts, is located at the crown

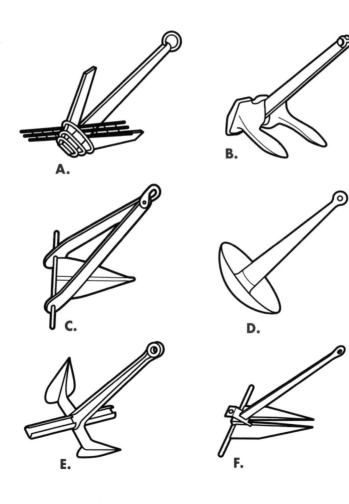

A.

B.

C.

D.

E.

F.

TATTOOS

Tattoos often have particular meaning to their bearers, but in maritime tradition some also have more general meaning. For example, sailors might bear different tattoos depending on places they have visited, distances they have travelled, or even as talismans to see them safely across the oceans.

Here are some specific examples of their meaning:

- **Pig tattooed on one foot, and a rooster on the other.** Said to protect a seaman from drowning. Typically, both animals would be kept in wooden crates on board navy ships. Crates would float in the event of the ship sinking, so sailors could grab hold for safety.

- **Fully rigged ship.** Shows the sailor has sailed round Cape Horn.

- **Anchor.** Shows the sailor has sailed the Atlantic Ocean.

- **Dragon.** Shows that the sailor has served on a China station.

- **Shellback turtle.** Shows the sailor has crossed the Equator.

- **Swallow.** Shows the sailor has travelled for 5,000 nautical miles.

- **'Hold' tattooed on the knuckles of one hand and 'Fast' on the other.** Said to allow the bearer to grip the rigging better.

Given the information on the previous page, can you match each of the tattooed arms shown below to one of the four sailors' quotes beneath? Not every sailor will bear every tattoo that applies to them, but the arms and quotes can be uniquely paired.

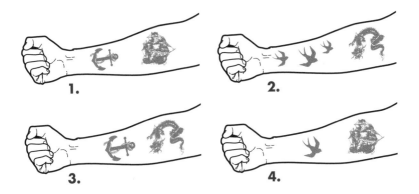

1.

2.

3.

4.

A. 'I've travelled over 8,000 nautical miles across the sea and fought tempestuous waters – travelling around Cape Horn was quite something!'

B. 'After leaving Shanghai, I found a crew and sailed to New Zealand. I've sailed at least 15,000 nautical miles.'

C. 'We set out from Bristol and navigated via Cape Horn.'

D. 'My voyages have taken me from Portugal to cross the oceans to America, and even as far as China.'

Bonus Question:
In 1909, a recruitment flyer for which country's navy required sailors with 'indecent or obscene tattooing' to alter them before being allowed to enlist?

NAVAL UNIFORMS

Uniform for officers in the Royal Navy was introduced in 1748. The design of uniform was adapted to reflect broad changes in male fashion. Different ranks were variously indicated by buttons, gold braid, epaulettes and other features. The National Maritime Museum uniform collection is over 7,000 items, including some owned by Admiral Nelson, Edward VII and Admiral John Arbuthnot Fisher. The oldest uniforms in the collection are of the first pattern, introduced in 1748.

1. Use the visual guide to identify the subjects of the portraits on the following pages. Their names and ranks are as follows:

   • Admiral of the Fleet John Jellicoe, 1st Earl Jellicoe
   • Captain Robert Scott
   • Rear-Admiral Sir Henry Codrington
   • Admiral Sir Arthur Moore
   • Admiral Sir John Fisher
   • Midshipman Robert Deans

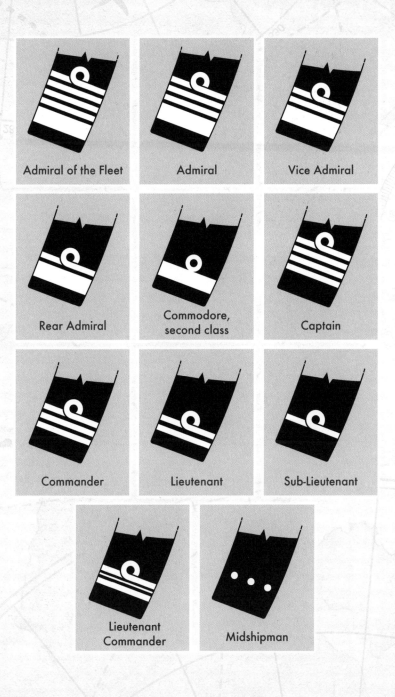

Admiral of the Fleet

Admiral

Vice Admiral

Rear Admiral

Commodore, second class

Captain

Commander

Lieutenant

Sub-Lieutenant

Lieutenant Commander

Midshipman

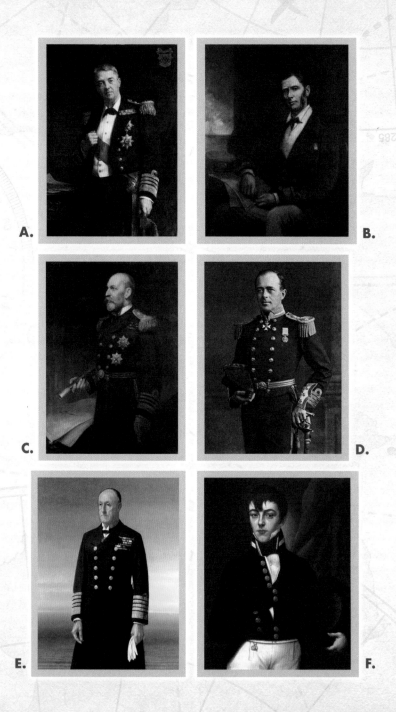

A.

B.

C.

D.

E.

F.

Once you have identified the people in each of the portraits, try the following questions:

2. Which of the portraits shows an officer wearing admiral's ball dress?

3. Which of the paintings shown do you think was painted first?

4. Which one of the illustrated men later became Governor-General of New Zealand?

5. Can you identify the object shown resting on top of the charts in portrait (c), and shown enlarged here?

6. Which feature of naval uniforms, shown in three of the portraits, was officially phased out in 1960?

7. What was the name given to Captain Robert Scott's ill-fated expedition to Antarctica? It translates to mean 'new land'.

OCCUPATIONAL BADGES

Occupational badges are used to indicate certain specialities within the Royal Navy, or to reveal the length of a sailor's service. To the side of each of the badges shown here, the name of the role it was once associated with has been given – but with all of its letters scrambled. Can you rearrange the letters and reveal the names of the occupations?

To help you, the number of words needed for each solution is shown in brackets beneath each anagram, as well as an indication of the field in which the role operates. The spacing in the anagrams doesn't necessarily correspond with that in the answer. You can also use the pictures on the badges to help you, of course.

1. LEG RUBS
(1 – Musical)

2. MAIN SLANG
(1 – Communications)

3. PLAIN ALCOVE
(2 – Law enforcement)

4. SLIGHT REPEAT
(1 – Communications)

5. RACKS FIFTH BEST
(3 – Medical)

6. SCRAPE WOOD TOXIN
(2 – Weaponry)

GANSEYS

Women knitting ganseys. The photograph was probably taken in Scarborough's harbour, c.1910.

Ganseys are tightly knitted jumpers traditionally worn by fishermen to help protect them from the elements while at sea. Each gansey had a distinctive pattern so that if its owner was to be lost at sea, it would be possible to identify their body from the pattern of their gansey. Patterns would be based on things that were important to their owner, perhaps representing rope, fish-bones, waves, lightning, nets and so on. A single wool was used for each jumper, so each was a single colour, such as navy blue or cream.

Now see if you can create a gansey pattern of your own by solving the puzzle opposite. Using a knitting needle and wool would be a little involved, so in this case all you need to do is shade certain squares according to the numeric clues:

- Each clue provides from left to right or from top to bottom, the length of each run of consecutive shaded squares in its row or column.

- If there is more than one run in a row or column then there must be at least one unshaded square between each run.

- All shaded squares are specified in the numeric clues, so all other squares must remain unshaded.

- A '0' clue means that there are no shaded squares in that row or column.

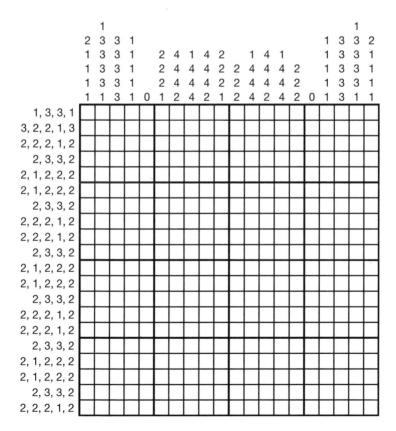

SHIPS' BADGES

Large, decorative badges started being attached to the hulls of warships in the nineteenth century in order to help more easily identify them. The symbols or pictures used on each badge were typically designed to reflect the name of the ship, and the shape of the badge would indicate the type of vessel:

- Circular badges represented battle ships and battle cruisers
- Shield-shaped badges indicated destroyers
- Pentagonal badges were used for cruisers
- Diamond-shaped badges were used generally for all other types of ship

The names of ten ships are given below, and the badges that belong to them are shown on the opposite page. Based on the images, and the labelling of cruisers and destroyers in the list below, can you match each name to its badge?

1. HMS *Curlew* (Cruiser)
2. HMS *Delhi* (Cruiser)
3. HMS *Malcolm* (Destroyer)
4. HMS *Trusty* (Destroyer)
5. HMS *Warwick* (Destroyer)
6. HMS *Bee*
7. HMS *Dryad*
8. HMS *Hermes*
9. HMS *Pandora*
10. HMS *Sandwich*

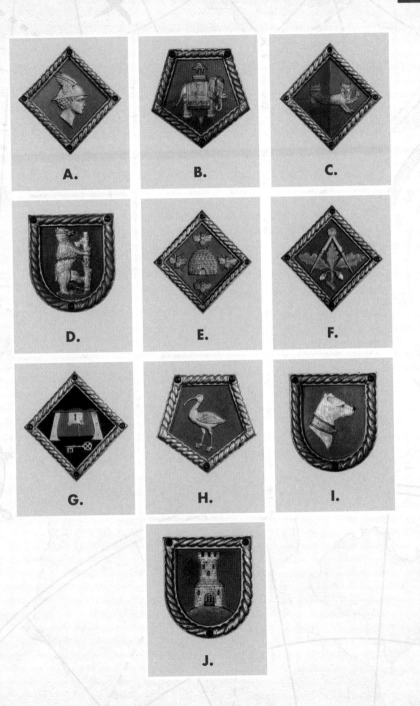

A.

B.

C.

D.

E.

F.

G.

H.

I.

J.

BROKEN BADGES

The ships' badges on the opposite page all include a single-word name of their ship at the top of the badge, but we have hidden part of each word. Each missing part is in fact a regular English word, which you can reveal by solving the word puzzles below.

In each puzzle, find the word you can place in the gap to form two further words by joining its letters to either the preceding or following word. For example, DOOR _ _ _ TRESS can be solved by filling with the word 'MAT', forming 'DOORMAT' and 'MATTRESS'. Each puzzle number corresponds to the badge of the same number opposite. Find the missing words and reveal each of the original ship names.

1. BOB   _ _ _   FISH

2. JOBS   _ _ _ _ _   WHILE

3. FLAG   _ _ _ _ _   MASON

4. TWO   _ _ _ _   AWAY

5. BRACE   _ _ _   DOWN

6. OFF   _ _ _ _ _   LINE

7. TAR   _ _ _   GOES

HOUSE FLAGS

House flags were first introduced in the late-eighteenth century. The flags on the following pages are all examples of house flags, used by organisations and trading companies to identify themselves at sea. Use the flag designs overleaf to answer the following questions.

Print showing the clipper ship Highflyer, *which was built by R. and H. Green at Blackwall in 1860 for their London to Australia run. The Blackwall Line house flag is at the mainsail.*

1. Using your common sense and general knowledge, can you identify which flag represented each of the following companies?

   a. British Rail
   b. British Waterways Board
   c. Canadian National Steamships
   d. Chevron Steamships
   e. Crusader Shipping
   f. North Yorkshire Shipping
   g. Royal Mail Lines
   h. Shell Tankers

2. Each of the clues below is describing a different word, which can be spelled using only the letters found on the house flags. No letter can be used more times than it appears across all of the flags. Can you solve every clue?

   a. The Suez and Panama are these
   b. A double-hulled boat
   c. Celestial bodies used for navigation at night
   d. Nautical maps
   e. Rocky waterfalls, famously found on the Nile
   f. Traders
   g. A spice mix from the Indian subcontinent

3.

a. What is the heraldic name given to the diagonal cross used by two of these flags?

b. Which country's national flag is often referred to simply by the answer to 'a'?

c. Based on the colours of the two diagonal crosses shown, can you guess from which two countries the companies they are associated with operate?

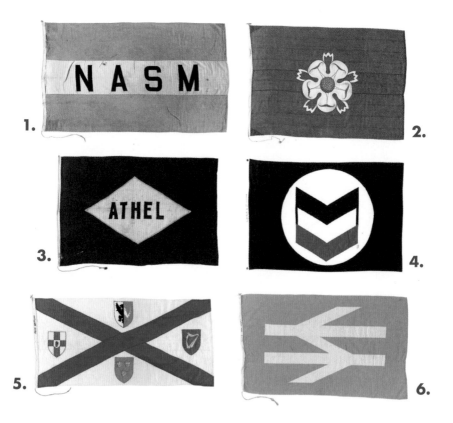

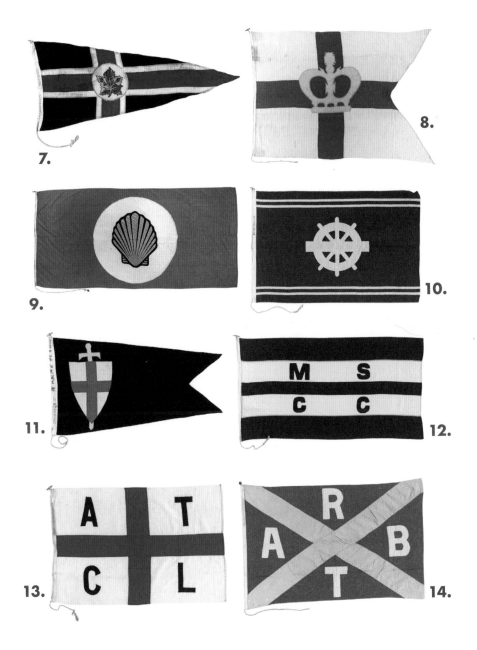

7.

8.

9.

10.

11.

12.

13.

14.

SIGNAL FLAGS

Signal flags represent the most important form of communication at sea. Each flag represents a single letter of the alphabet, as well as a specific message or meaning, such as 'man overboard' or 'I require assistance'.

SIGNAL FLAGS FOR A TO Z

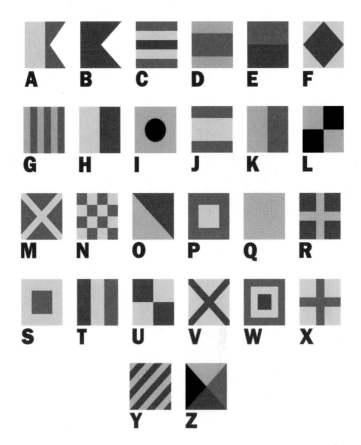

1. The names of six types of flag have been encoded below using international maritime signal flags. Using the guide shown, can you reveal each of the names?

a.

b.

c.

d.

e.

f.

2. Once you have revealed the names of the encoded flags, can you assign each of these six types of flag to one of the functions below? Two additional functions will remain unused.

    a. Flown as a polite greeting to a passing ship
    b. Flown to invite officers from other ships on board for a drink
    c. Flown to show that a religious service is happening on board
    d. Flown in the Royal Navy to show that an admiral is on board
    e. Flown at the bow when a ship is moored or at anchor
    f. Flown by a ship that is visiting foreign waters
    g. Flown to show that the ship is sailing at full speed
    h. Flown at the stern to indicate the nationality of a ship

UNION JACK

The Union Jack is the name given to the flag of the United Kingdom, which is notable for its inclusion of symbolic elements from the flags of three of the four countries that historically formed the union. Scotland is represented by a white saltire (diagonal cross) on a blue field (an area with a single background colour), Ireland by an overlaid red saltire, and England by a red and white cross. Wales is absent from the flag.

Can you answer the following questions about the Union Jack, its history and its modern usage?

1. Why is Wales absent from the flag?

2. Which Commonwealth nation refers to the Union Jack as the Royal Union Flag?

3. Which US state features the Union Jack in its state flag, as shown below?

4. Can you identify the countries represented by the following national flags, all of which include the Union Jack?

a.   b.

c.   d.

5. Flying the Union Jack upside down, especially at sea, is considered to be a coded signal. What does it indicate?

6. The United Kingdom was formed in stages. The Acts of Union in 1707 joined together the kingdoms of England (with Wales) and Scotland to form the United Kingdom, and the Act of Union in 1800 joined Ireland with Great Britain to form the United Kingdom of Great Britain and Ireland, with effect from 1801. Based on the information already given about the symbolic elements of the Union Jack, to what century can you date the flag shown below?

SEMAPHORE

A sketch of a seaman with semaphore flags by William Lionel Wyllie.

Semaphore – the use of flags to spell out messages – is still used in the nautical world today as a means of communication. Two flags are held up simultaneously by a signalman, with the position of the two flags relative to the position of the signalman indicating a single letter of the alphabet. When the two flags are moved to a new position, a second letter is spelled out, and so on. In this way, whole words can be spelled out letter by letter.

Using the guide on the opposite page, can you decipher the words spelled out in semaphore below it, all of which follow a nautical theme?

MORSE CODE

For many years the Morse code message for 'SOS' was used as a distress signal for ships of all sizes: dot dot dot, dash dash dash, dot dot dot. Although Morse code is now rarely used for modern communication, it still remains the best-known method for encrypting messages via a simple on/off system. Messages can be sent via wires or over radio as clicks or other sounds, visually as flashes of light, or indeed via a range of other methods.

Using the guide to Morse code opposite, can you decode each of the phrases below? All of the phrases have a nautical origin – except one. Can you also spot the odd one out? The slashes are used to indicate gaps between words.

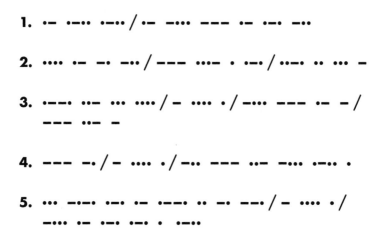

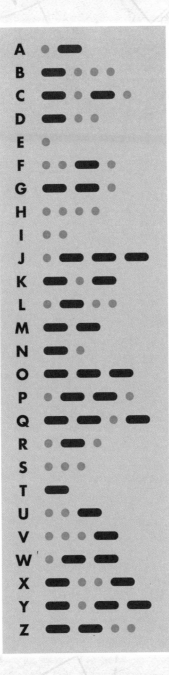

LIGHTHOUSES – Mapping the Beacons

Travelling the seas exposes sailors to a long list of risks. Seafarers have over time used many different instruments to help them find their way, such as chronometers, radios, satellite navigation and even the stars. Nearer to shore, lighthouses have since ancient times also helped ships navigate safely by making dangerous coastal areas more visible, and marking places of safe entry to harbours. Not all lighthouses need to be on the shore, however, since innovative ways of building have been developed over the years to allow lighthouses to be built on remote rocks, often in inhospitable conditions.

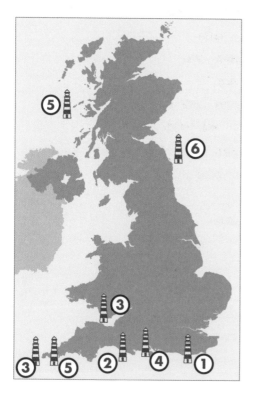

The locations of eight lighthouses are marked on this map, but their names have been encoded opposite using a simple alphabet-shift cipher. In this cipher, each letter in a name has been shifted forward a fixed number of positions in the alphabet. For example, LIGHTHOUSE with each letter shifted forward by two would become NKIJVJQWUG.

The numbers on the map reveal how many letters forward each lighthouse's name has been shifted. By using these shifts, and the descriptions below, can you reveal the name of each of the labelled lighthouses?

A. CFBDIZ IFBE

This offshore lighthouse is located near a well-known headland

B. XPJWWDATWJ

This lighthouse is the tallest in its country

C. ZROI URFN

This lighthouse bears a lupine name

D. QNEFWI

This lighthouse can be found at an extreme of a compass point in mainland Britain

E. RIIHPIW

This lighthouse is located on a well-known geological formation

F. RQTVNCPF DKNN

This lighthouse used to be divided into two parts called the Old Higher Lighthouse and Old Lower Lighthouse

G. QDVK SRLQW

This lighthouse was the last in its country to be made automatic

H. RUTMYZUTK

This lighthouse was once home to Grace Darling, famous for her role in rescuing sailors from the *Forfarshire*

EDDYSTONE LIGHTHOUSE

The original Eddystone tower, built on a small and dangerous rock 13 miles south-west of Plymouth in 1698.

The most famous lighthouse in the British Isles is probably the Eddystone, originally designed by Henry Winstanley. It was the first lighthouse to be built on a small rock in the open sea. There have been four separate lighthouses built here. A second structure made of concrete, brick and wood was built in the early eighteenth century after the original tower was destroyed in the Great Storm of 1703. This lasted fifty years, until it caught fire and burned down.

The third lighthouse was considered a major step forward in term of its design, with a new type of concrete, and its upper part still forms part of a monument in Plymouth. Finally, the current lighthouse was completed in 1881 and is still in use today, operated from a control centre in Essex.

Can you answer the following multiple-choice questions on the history of the Eddystone Lighthouse?

1. Where does the name 'Eddystone' come from?
   a. Its original patron
   b. The rocks it is built on
   c. The type of material it was first built from

2. What did the builder of the third version of the lighthouse, John Smeaton, give to each of the construction workers at the lighthouse to prevent them being press-ganged into recruitment to the Navy?

a. A letter of authentication
b. A hat
c. A medal

3. What did Smeaton base the shape of his Eddystone Lighthouse on?
   a. A Greek column
   b. An oak tree
   c. Chalk formations

4. Which of the following inspired Smeaton's plan for how to lay the stones in the building of the lighthouse?
   a. Snake scales
   b. London kerbstones
   c. Stepping stones

5. Henry Winstanley, the first person to build a lighthouse at Eddystone, was abducted by a privateer from which nation during the lighthouse's construction in the seventeenth century?
   a. France
   b. The Netherlands
   c. Spain

6. Which nautical novel, published in 1851, references the Eddystone Lighthouse?
   a. Treasure Island
   b. Moby Dick
   c. Lord Jim

7. Which multinational corporation celebrated the 321st anniversary of the Eddystone Lighthouse in 2019?
   a. Microsoft
   b. Facebook
   c. Google

THE SHIPPING FORECAST

The maritime area around the British Isles is divided into distinct, named zones, which are used in the broadcast of the shipping forecast each day. Each of these sea areas is marked on the map opposite, but some of the names have been replaced with letters.

1. Can you match the names of the areas below with each of the unnamed areas marked with a single letter on the map?

- Biscay
- Faeroes
- Forth
- German Bight
- Hebrides
- Humber
- Irish Sea
- Shannon
- Southeast Iceland
- Thames
- Tyne
- Viking
- Wight

2. How many of the twenty-six areas are named after estuaries?

3. Viking, Bailey and Sole are all named after a particular maritime geographical feature.
  a. What is the name of this type of feature?
  b. Can you name the other three sea areas named after the same kind of feature?

4. Which of the sea areas is named after the captain of HMS *Beagle*?

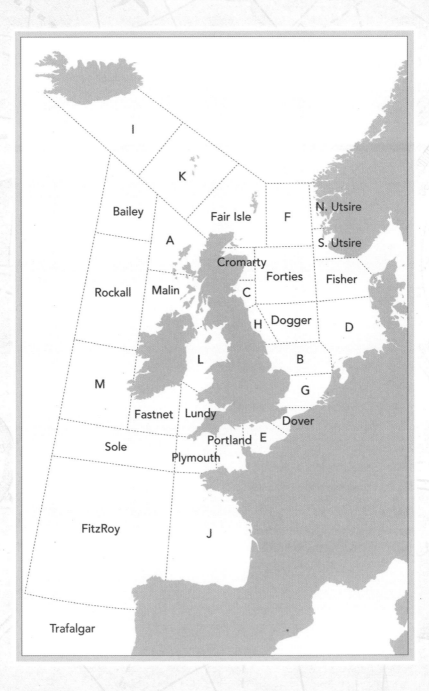

NAVIGATIONAL TOOLS

With over two thirds of the globe covered by water, it has been essential throughout history to navigate safely and effectively over the sea. Seafarers have used a number of tools to assist with this, which have improved in effectivity since the sixteenth century. On the opposite page are six instruments used at sea to aid seafarers in finding their location. Can you match each instrument with its dates of provenance and the description of its functions below?

1. DATE: around 1725
Used to help with drawing parallel lines precisely

2. DATE: around 1800
Used for viewing objects more closely while out at sea

3. DATE: around 1800
Used for measuring air pressure

4. DATE: around 1588
Used for measuring the altitude above the horizon of stars and the Sun

5. DATE: around 1798
Used to measure altitudes and angular distances between objects

6. DATE: around 1830
Used to determine the position of a ship on a chart in relation to two landmarks

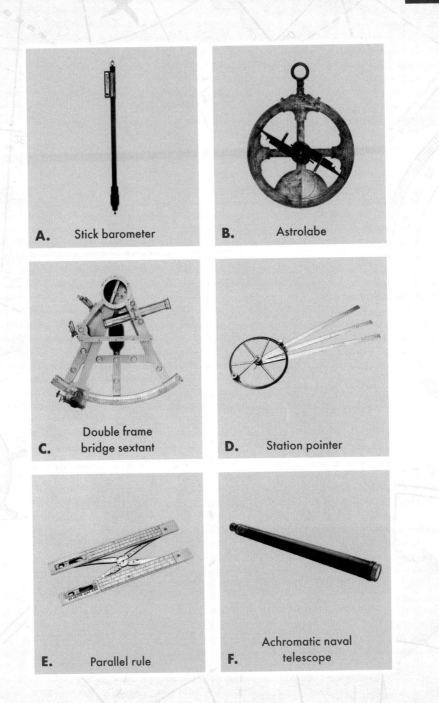

A.   Stick barometer

B.   Astrolabe

C.   Double frame bridge sextant

D.   Station pointer

E.   Parallel rule

F.   Achromatic naval telescope

SOLUTIONS

Anchor Names
1. STONE AND ROPE
2. PRIMITIVE
3. EAST INDIAN
4. ADMIRALTY
5. PLOUGH
6. PORTER
Bonus Question: A fouled anchor.

Anchor Parts
1. Stockless – **B**
2. Wishbone – **C**
3. Mushroom – **D**
4. Northill – **E**
5. Danforth – **F**
6. Chinese – **A**

Tattoos

Arm	Quote
1	C
2	B
3	D
4	A

Bonus Question: The US Navy

Naval Uniforms
1.
    a. Admiral Sir John Fisher
    b. Rear-Admiral Sir Henry Codrington

    c. Admiral Sir Arthur Moore

    d. Captain Robert Scott

    e. Admiral of the Fleet John Jellicoe

    f. Midshipman Robert Deans

2. The portrait of Admiral Sir John Fisher (a)

3. The portrait of Midshipman Robert Deans (f) is the oldest. It was painted in 1807.

4. Admiral of the Fleet John Jellicoe, 1st Earl Jellicoe (e). He became Australia's second Governor-General in 1920.

5. It is a divider, used to measure map distance.

6. Epaulettes, which can be seen in (a), (c) and (d)

7. The *Terra Nova* expedition.

Occupational Badges

1. BUGLERS

2. SIGNALMAN

3. NAVAL POLICE

4. TELEGRAPHIST

5. SICK BERTH STAFF

6. TORPEDO COXSWAIN

Ganseys

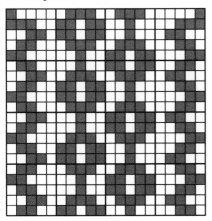

Ships' Badges

HMS *Curlew* – **H**

HMS *Delhi* – **B**

HMS *Malcolm* – **J**

HMS *Trusty* – **I**

HMS *Warwick* – **D**

HMS *Bee* – **E**

HMS *Dryad* – **F**

HMS *Hermes* – **A**

HMS *Pandora* – **G**

HMS *Sandwich* – **C**

Broken Badges

1. CAT: BOBCAT and CATFISH, making the ship name CATTISTOCK
2. WORTH: JOBSWORTH and WORTHWHILE, making the ship name HURWORTH
3. STONE: FLAGSTONE and STONEMASON, making the ship name ATHERSTONE
4. FOLD: TWOFOLD and FOLDAWAY, making the ship name CHIDDINGFOLD
5. LET: BRACELET and LETDOWN, making the ship name MIDDLETON
6. SHORE: OFFSHORE and SHORELINE, making the ship name SHOREHAM
7. TAN: TARTAN and TANGOES, making the ship name SULTAN

House Flags

1.
   a. British Rail – **6**
   b. British Waterways Board – **10**
   c. Canadian National Steamships – **7**
   d. Chevron Steamships – **4**

    e. Crusader Shipping – **11**
    f. North Yorkshire Shipping – **2**
    g. Royal Mail Lines – **8**
    h. Shell Tankers – **9**

2.

    a. CANALS
    b. CATAMARAN
    c. STARS
    d. CHARTS
    e. CATARACTS
    f. MERCHANTS
    g. MASALA

3.

    a. A saltire.
    b. The flag of Scotland, featuring a white saltire on a blue background, is often referred to simply as 'The Saltire'.
    c. The red saltire on a white background depicts an Irish company (Irish Shipping), and the yellow saltire on a blue background represents a Swedish company (Rederiaktiebolaget Transatlantic).

Signal Flags

1.

    a. Jack
    b. Ensign
    c. St George's Cross
    d. Church pennant
    e. Gin pennant
    f. Courtesy flag

2.

a. Jack – e) flown at the bow when a ship is moored or at anchor

b. Ensign – h) flown at the stern to indicate the nationality of a ship

c. St George's Cross – d) flown in the Royal Navy to show that an admiral is on board

d. Church pennant – c) flown to show that a religious service is happening on board

e. Gin pennant – b) flown to invite officers from other ships on board for a drink

f. Courtesy flag – f) flown by a ship that is visiting foreign waters

Union Jack

1. Wales. The presence of Wales on the flag is implied by the red cross of England, as Wales and England were already considered one kingdom – after the annexation of Wales by England in the thirteenth century – prior to the union with Scotland in 1707.

2. Canada

3. Hawaii

4. The countries represented by the flags are:

   a. New Zealand

   b. Australia

   c. Fiji

   d. Tuvalu

5. Flying the Union Jack upside down is considered to be a distress signal, although it can also be a sign of mere incompetence!

6. The eighteenth century, since it postdates 1701 and predates 1800, given the presence of all modern elements except for the red saltire of Ireland.

Semaphore
1. LIGHTHOUSE
2. ANCHOR
3. MARITIME
4. ADMIRAL

Morse Code
1. ALL ABOARD
2. HAND OVER FIST
3. PUSH THE BOAT OUT
4. ON THE DOUBLE
5. SCRAPING THE BARREL

'On the double' is the odd phrase out – its origins are in the army, relating to the speed at which troops march.

Lighthouses – Mapping the Beacons
A. BEACHY HEAD, located on the south coast just east of Brighton, shift: 1
B. SKERRYVORE, located off the west coast of Scotland, shift: 5
C. WOLF ROCK, located between Penzance and the Isles of Scilly, shift: 3
D. LIZARD, located on the south coast of Cornwall, shift: 5
E. NEEDLES, located off the west coast of the Isle of Wight, shift: 4
F. PORTLAND BILL, located on the south coast just west of Bournemouth, shift: 2
G. NASH POINT, located on the south coast of Wales, shift: 3
H. LONGSTONE, located off the Northumberland coast, shift: 6

Eddystone Lighthouse

1. b. The rocks it is built on
2. c. A medal
3. b. An oak tree
4. b. London kerbstones
5. a. France
6. b. *Moby Dick*
7. c. Google, with a Google Doodle

The Shipping Forecast

1. The names correspond to the following labels on the map:
- Biscay – J
- Faeroes – K
- Forth – C
- German Bight – D
- Hebrides – A
- Humber – B
- Irish Sea – L
- Shannon – M
- Southeast Iceland – I
- Thames – G
- Tyne – H
- Viking – F
- Wight – E

2. Six – Thames, Humber, Tyne, Forth, Cromarty and Shannon.

3. **a.** Sandbanks.

 b. The other areas named after sandbanks (also known as sandbars) are Dogger, Forties and Fisher.

4. FitzRoy. The area was previously known as Finisterre but was changed in 2002 to commemorate Vice-Admiral Robert FitzRoy.

Navigational Tools

1. Parallel rule – **E**
2. Achromatic naval telescope – **F**
3. Stick barometer – **A**
4. Astrolabe – **B**
5. Double frame bridge sextant – **C**
6. Station pointer – **D**

CHAPTER 2

SHIPSHAPE

Think you know your canoes from your catamarans? A clipper from a cutter? This chapter is inspired by all kinds of vessels, and their many uses and histories. It's a chance to unpick exactly what the difference is between a ship and a boat* and to find out some fascinating facts about shipping and famous ships along the way.

* A common definition is that a boat can be carried on a ship. But if a ship has to be carried on a ship-carrier, that does not make it a boat…

TYPES OF SHIP – Ship Code

Over time, vessels have developed to suit particular tasks, different sea conditions and the patterns of local tradition. The number of masts, the position of the rigging, the length of the keel and how many decks the ship has, will determine whether it's a ketch, a dhow or a host of other vessel types.

Reveal the names of ten different types of vessel by cracking the number code, in which each letter has been replaced by a number. You can use the descriptive clues to help you, along with your puzzle-solving skills. A grid is provided for you to keep track of your deductions, and two letters are already solved to get you started.

1. A type of sailing boat with one mast

13	8	11 ⭕	11 ⭕	2

2. A sailing ship with a minimum of two masts

13	14	17	11 ⭕	11 ⭕	6	10	7

3. A speedy ship, first built to transport cargo in the mid-nineteenth century

14	8	19	2	2	10	7

4. A sailboat designed for speed

14	5	16	16	10	7

5. A Portuguese sailing ship first built in the fifteenth century

14	3	7	3	20	10	8

6. A warship, used by modern navies to escort other ships

15	7	19	4 G	3	16	10

7. Sir Francis Drake's ship, *Golden Hind* is an example of this kind of ship

4 G	3	8	8	10	11 O	6

8. A type of sailing ship that usually has three masts

9	3	7	18	5	10

9. A sailing ship developed in China

12	5	6	1

10. A type of small, armed naval ship

4 G	5	6	9	11 O	3	16

1	2	3	4	5	6	7	8	9	10	11	12	13	14	15	16	17	18	19	20
			G							O									

MULTI-HULL BOATS

Various vessels, from traditional Pacific craft to some modern racing yachts, are multi-hulled. The principal reason for more than one hull is that it allows the vessel to employ a larger surface area of sail, i.e., catching more wind, while remaining stable in the water.

The following images show the basic appearance of six different types of boat when viewed from beneath. In this puzzle, we have assigned each of these types of boat a brief descriptive code. Can you work out how this code works, and then decide which boat each of these refers to?

1. H1

2. H1O1B2

3. H1O2B4

4. H1SH1B3

5. H2B2

6. H1SH2B4

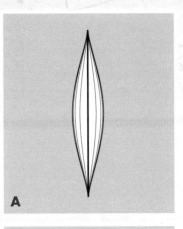

A

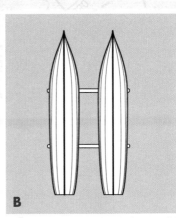

B

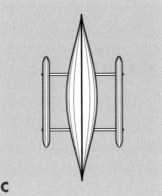

C

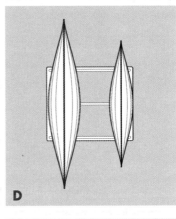

D

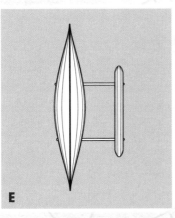

E

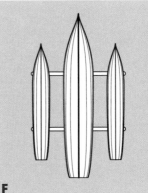

F

SHIPBUILDING MATERIALS

Hidden in this jumble of letters are types of wood and other raw materials that were used for building different parts of a ship, or for making objects used on a ship. There are six in total – can you find them all, and assign each word to one of the six empty slots below, based on what the material was used for?

HULL PLANKS   •...

OTHER PLANKS   •...

•...

MAST   •...

SAILS AND ROPE   •...

•...

SHIPBUILDERS

The titles of six jobs involved in sixteenth-century shipbuilding have been split up into fragments, and then those fragments have been rearranged.

Can you place the fragments back together, and reveal the six different jobs?

CAR	CAU	ER	GER
GHT	JOI	KER	LK
LMA	NER	PEN	RIG
SAI	SHIP	TER	WRI

Shipbuilding *by Henry Rushbury, 1944.*

PARTS OF A SHIP

Complete this empty crossword grid by fitting the names of various ship parts into it, with one letter per square so every square is used. Not every label on the ship has a place in the crossword – one label will remain unused once the grid is filled. No word is used more than once, and words should be placed exactly as written (including preserving singular/plural forms).

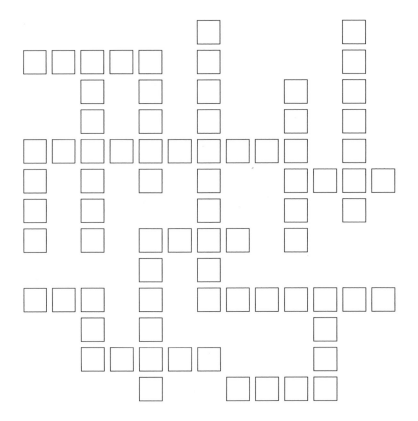

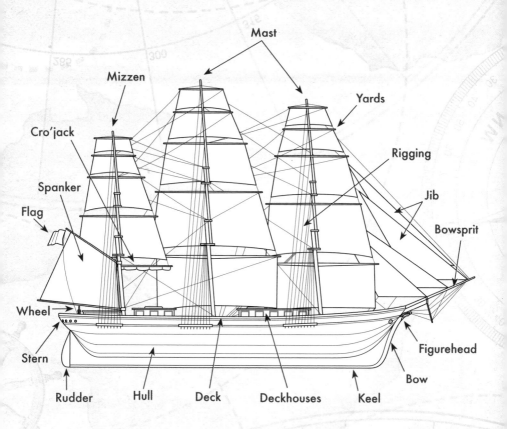

Mast

Mizzen

Cro'jack

Yards

Spanker

Rigging

Flag

Jib

Bowsprit

Wheel

Figurehead

Stern

Bow

Rudder   Hull   Deck   Deckhouses   Keel

FIGUREHEADS

The National Maritime Museum holds the largest collection of ships' figureheads in the world. The origins of the figurehead lie far back in the pre-historic past. Some cultures decorated their simple vessels with painted eyes to help them 'see' their way safely through the water. At its most basic, a figurehead is simply a device at the upper extremity of the stem-post at the bow of the vessel.

The initial inspiration for figureheads was, therefore, a mixture of practical decoration to this exposed end of a timber and some form of symbolism, religious or spiritual, to provide protection, ensuring a safe passage for people and goods. However, more robust and varied carvings were added as ship designs changed.

The following clues reveal information about the identities of the characters depicted on the figureheads overleaf. Using as few clues as possible from each set, can you both identify the people and match them to their carved depictions? Four of the people are real historical figures, but the fifth is purely fictional.

1. **SHE:**
   - is named after the city in which she was born
   - established one of the first formal schools of nursing
   - is best known for her work during the Crimean War
   - is sometimes known as 'The Lady with the Lamp'

2. **HE:**
   - was a close friend of William Pitt the Younger
   - is buried at Westminster Abbey
   - was the Member of Parliament for Yorkshire from 1784–1812
   - was a key figure in the movement for the abolition of slavery

3. HE:

- suffered from seasickness
- was a Vice-Admiral in the Royal Navy
- is commemorated with a statue in Trafalgar Square
- died on board the *Victory* during the Battle of Trafalgar

4. HE:

- was born in Kentucky in 1809
- was the sixteenth president of the United States of America
- was assassinated in 1865
- issued the Emancipation Proclamation to bring about the emancipation of slaves in the USA

5. SHE:

- wears a garment that gives its name to the ship that the figurehead is found on
- is a legendary Scottish witch
- features in Robert Burns' poem *Tam o' Shanter*
- is depicted holding the tail of the protagonist Tam's horse

Bonus Question:

Can you also guess the names of the ships that the figureheads come from?

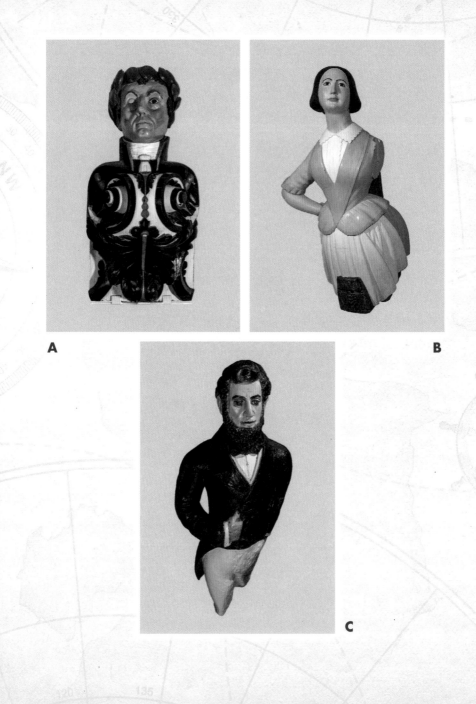

A

B

C

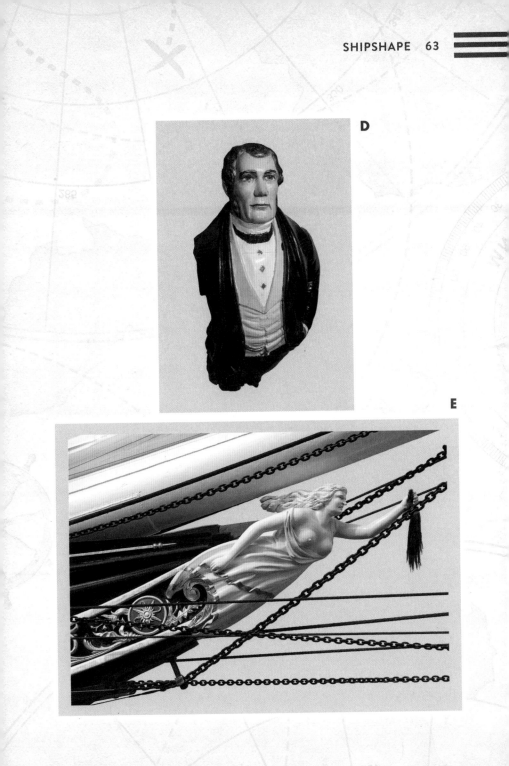

D

E

SAILS

The names of some sails that could be rigged on a clipper vessel have been listed opposite, each accompanied by a letter.

Use the descriptions to work out which sail is which, and copy each sail's corresponding letter into the circle at its bottom-left corner. Once complete, the letters will spell out a nautical expression when read from left to right and top to bottom.

- The ship has three masts, which in order from bow to stern are the *fore*, *main*, and *mizzen* masts
- The spanker is the sternmost sail on this ship
- The topsail is above the course, and below the topgallant
- The mainmast also has a skysail, which is rigged at the top of the mast
- Where the main and foresails have a course, the mizzen has a cro'jack
- The royal sail is rigged at the top of the fore and mizzen masts
- The jib can be found at the bow

A	–	Fore Topsail
A	–	Main Skysail
I	–	Mizzen Topsail
M	–	Flying Jib
N	–	Main Topsail
N	–	Mizzen Royal
O	–	Main Course
O	–	Mizzen Topgallant
P	–	Fore Royal
R	–	Fore Course
R	–	Main Topgallant
S	–	Spanker
T	–	Cro'jack
T	–	Fore Topgallant
Y	–	Main Royal

KNOTS

The following illustrations show six of a sailor's most useful knots:

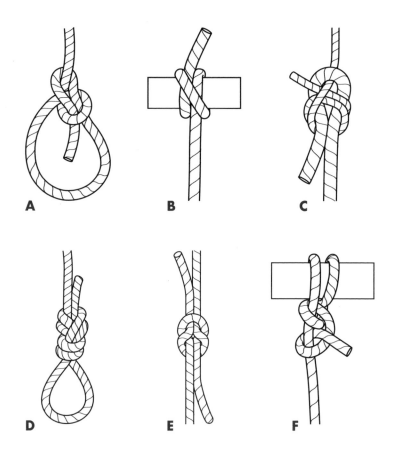

Based on the descriptions that follow, can you work out the name of each of the knots? Each description includes a step-by-step guide to tying the particular knot.

FIGURE OF EIGHT

This is known as a 'stopper knot', as it prevents a length of rope passing through a block or cleat when you don't want it to. It can also be used to create a loop very quickly. It is commonly used on the mainsheet and jib sheet on sailing boats so that you don't lose the end of the rope (the 'sheet' is the name of the rope used to control the sails).

1. Take an end of the rope in each hand.
2. Pass the end over the top of the rope to create a loop.
3. Pass the loop over the top of the two pieces of rope to create a new loop of double rope at the bottom.
4. Pass the end with the single loop under the rope in the hand.
5. Bring the single loop back up and pass down through the double rope loop.
6. Pull tight.

REEF KNOT

Historically this knot was used when the sails were reefed (made smaller) by gathering up the bottom of the sail using ropes passed through it at regular intervals. The ends of each rope were then tied together to keep the bottom of the sail rolled up in stormy weather. A reefed vessel is safer to sail in strong winds.

1. Take an end of the rope in each hand.
2. Pass the left end over the right end and under, just like the first step of tying a shoelace.
3. Then pass the end now on the left over the right and under.
4. When pulled together the knot should be symmetrical and tidy. The rope should come out on the top or on the bottom at each end of the knot.

ROUND TURN AND TWO HALF HITCHES

This knot is used for tying up boats where the knot needs to be untied while the rope is still under some pressure. It is useful for tying around posts or rings.

1. Pass one end of the rope through or around an object, like a pole.
2. Pass it around again without crossing it over the first turn to create the round turn.
3. Take the long end of the rope in one hand and the shorter end in the other.
4. Now take the shorter end over the other part of the rope close to the object and pass the end through the loop you have just made to create the first half hitch.
5. Repeat the same process as step 4 to create the second half hitch.

CLOVE HITCH

The clove hitch is a good knot for securing a boat to a railing, post or similar object.

1. Pass the end of the rope over the post (or similar) and back around, crossing over the other end of the rope.
2. Continue to take the end of the rope over the post loosely, creating a loop.
3. Pass the end of the rope around the back of the post and through the loop.
4. Pull tight.

BOWLINE

This is an excellent knot as it does not slip easily. It is useful for towing another boat or tying two bits of rope together.

1. Hold the length of rope in one hand, and with your other hand, part of the way up the rope from the end, create a small loop by twisting the rope over itself. Clamp the rope at the twist with your thumb to stop the rope from falling out.
2. Next, bring the end of the rope up through the small loop from behind.
3. Take it around the back of the rope above your small loop, creating a larger loop below it.
4. When you have brought enough of the rope through the small loop and around the back of the rope, pass the end down through the small loop again.
5. Pull the rope tight above the small loop and the two ends of the rope passed through the small loop.

DOUBLE SHEET BEND

This is a stronger and more secure knot than a single sheet bend. It is used to join two pieces of rope together, especially of different thicknesses.

1. Create a 'U' shape in a piece of rope. This is called a 'bight'.
2. Pass the end of the second piece of rope up through the bight from underneath.
3. Continue to pass the rope around the back of the two ends of the first piece of rope.
4. Then pass the end of that rope under itself where it came up from below the bight. If you pull it tight now you will create a single sheet bend.
5. With the second piece of rope, complete another turn around the back of the bight and back under itself like the first time for a double sheet bend.
6. Pull tight.

CUTTY SARK CROSSWORD

Cutty Sark is the world's sole surviving tea clipper and is now an award-winning visitor attraction, following extensive restoration. The ship was built with one purpose – to bring tea from China back to London. It was the fastest of its time, returning from Australia to London in just 84 days on its first voyage to Australia in 1883. In 2019 the ship celebrated its 150th birthday, an incredible achievement considering few clippers lasted more than 20 years.

Test your knowledge of Cutty Sark by solving this crossword where all of the clues are related to the famous ship. Once complete, the letters in the highlighted squares can be anagrammed to spell out the name of a country that was frequently visited by the ship.

Cutty Sark welcomes over 270,000 visitors on board every year.

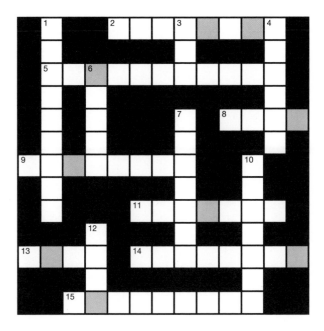

ACROSS

2 Its capital is Lisbon, home of the company that purchased *Cutty Sark* in the mid-1890s (8)

5 The process *Cutty Sark* underwent in 2012 (11)

8 Fleecy product, which *Cutty Sark* began transporting in the late 1800s (4)

9 Major Chinese city, destination of *Cutty Sark*'s first voyage (8)

11 Person in command of a ship (7)

13 Alcoholic drink, part of *Cutty Sark*'s cargo on its first voyage (4)

14 The name given to *Cutty Sark* during its time in 2–across (8)

15 Borough of 4–down where *Cutty Sark* is permanently moored (9)

DOWN

1 A vessel that carries goods, such as *Cutty Sark* (5, 4)

3 Product that *Cutty Sark* collected from China (3)

4 British city where *Cutty Sark* is located (6)

6 Number of captains *Cutty Sark* had during its 25 years as part of the British merchant fleet (5)

7 The type of ship *Cutty Sark* is (7)

10 Nationality that *Cutty Sark* regained in 1923 (7)

12 Alcoholic drink, part of *Cutty Sark*'s cargo on its first voyage (4)

CARGO PAIRS

Cutty Sark, *seen here loading wool at Circular Quay, Sydney, c.1883–1894.*

Wool was one of Australia's main exports to Britain and many ships made regular trips between London and Sydney or Melbourne. The Australian industry, specialising in Merino wool, had been expanding rapidly since its foundation in the early 1800s and by 1870 it was the world's largest producer of wool.

Cutty Sark is best known as a 'tea clipper', although tea is not the only commodity that it transported. Opposite is a list of various cargoes that Cutty Sark carried over its career, which have all been encoded. Delete one letter from each pair to reveal each of these different types of cargo. The first is done as an example, to reveal 'TEA'.

~~ST~~ ~~OE~~ A~~L~~

RW OP GO LU

PW AI NM TE

RC OH EA LN

HL LO DP SE

MS PO BI RE SI TP ES

WJ UE LT EK

FC AI NR DE LR ES YS

PC OA SE TW OE TR   MO EI SL

GS RA RA VD IY NC EU PS

HMS *BELFAST*

HMS Belfast *in 1938, stopped at Spithead with all guns trained to starboard.*

This puzzle takes you on a journey through HMS *Belfast*, a light cruiser that served in the Royal Navy from 1939 through until 1963. A portion of the plan for the ship can be found overleaf, showing individual rooms and decks.

Follow the instructions opposite to navigate around the ship and answer two specific questions. To navigate, assume that any instructions to move 'up' or 'down' mean 'travel vertically' on the plan, as stairs have not been labelled. Equally, you should assume that you can travel horizontally along a deck from any one room to another.

1.

- Begin in a room on the Forecastle where you might be likely to find a cabbage.
- Climb up two decks to the Lower Bridge and travel to the room closest to the stern on this level for a wash.
- Once you are clean, go up to the Compass Platform and find a room where strategy meetings might take place.
- From here, travel towards the bow until you reach a room where the ship can be commanded, whose name includes the position of a high-ranking officer.
- What could you have mended for you in a room two decks directly beneath your position?

2.

- Start close to the bow of the ship, in a room where you might be able to pick up some equipment for an expedition to the North Pole.
- Head down to a room where you may be able to purchase decorating supplies on the Upper Deck.
- From here, walk towards the stern until you are in a room where you can both relax and collect clothes.
- Go to the room beneath your current position on the Lower Deck to a storage room where you might find both clothing and cooking supplies.
- Walk towards the stern through a room where you might find a store of guns.
- As you continue into the next room on the same level, what might you notice about the temperature?

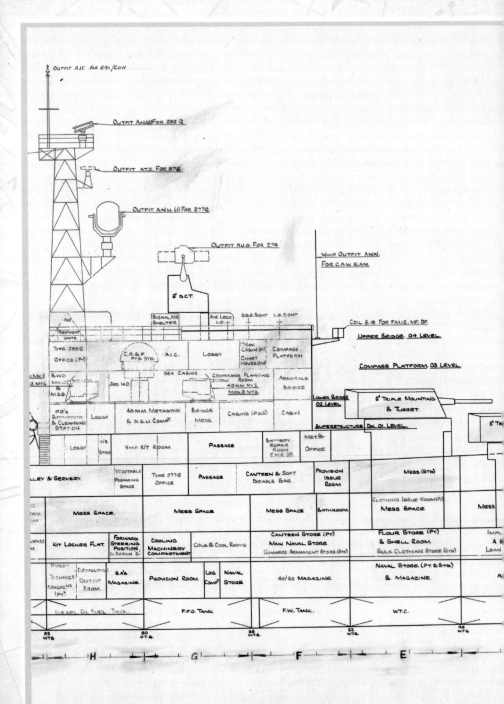

HMS *BELFAST*

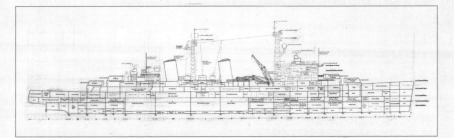

Complete profile of the ship plan for HMS Belfast.

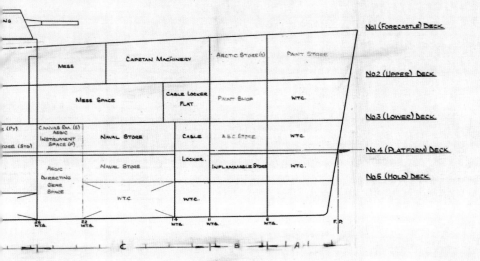

No1 (Forecastle) Deck

No2 (Upper) Deck

No3 (Lower) Deck

No4 (Platform) Deck

No5 (Hold) Deck

SHIP NAMING

The name of the historic sailing ship Cutty Sark *derives from the nickname for the fictional character Nannie Dee, a witch in the poem* Tam o'Shanter *by Robert Burns. Nannie wore a 'cutty sark' (short skirt).*

Ship names are often more meaningful than they might at first appear. For example, ships in the same class often share a theme, such as all being named after weapons, even if that theme has nothing directly to do with the class itself. A repeated initial letter is also often used for ships in the same class, as for example can be seen in the *Brazen*, *Bulldog* and *Boadicea*, all B-class ships built in the early twentieth century.

SHIP NAMING – MISSING VOWELS

The names of these eighteenth-century ships have had all of their vowels removed. Each of the names belongs to one of the categories used in ship naming by the Royal Navy at this time. Can you restore the vowels to reveal the names, and then work out what the categories were? Three different categories are used in this puzzle.

LZBTH	GMMNN	MNTR
XFRD	SSX	MRY
RYL NN	RYL WLLM	NPTN
SFFLK	YRK	JX
RYL GRG	NTTNGHM	MRS

SHIP NAMING – SHIP CLASSES

The names of four ships from each of three different classes are described by the definitions below. Can you work out the ship names, and then deduce what the naming pattern of each class is? The type of ship is given at the top of each list. The number of letters in each ship name is also given, omitting all ship prefixes (e.g., HMS).

Early 20th-Century

Destroyers

- Saint associated with love and romance (9)
- Scandinavian mythological handmaiden who escorted warriors to Valhalla (8)
- Heroic (8)
- Undead figure who feeds on blood (7)

Modern Navy

Destroyers

- Adventurous (6)
- Famously hard precious stone (7)
- Mythical reptile (6)
- Protector (8)

World War II

Corvettes*

- Winter-flowering plant with white blooms (8)
- Brightly coloured flower associated with the Netherlands (5)
- Tall, yellow-flowered plant with edible seeds (9)
- Daffodil-like plant; beautiful youth who fell in love with his own reflection (9)

* Corvettes in this context are small warships, not a type of car

Bonus Question:

What traditionally happens at the bow of a ship during its naming ceremony?

HMS Victory, renowned for being Lord Nelson's flagship in the Battle of Trafalgar, in 1805

COMMERCIAL SHIPPING – Hidden Port

An illustration of Chinese tea being unloaded in the London Docks.

Facts about five different port cities are listed below. Identify the ports and write their names into the boxes. Once all of the ports have been filled in, a sixth will be spelled out in the highlighted boxes, reading from top to bottom.

1.

- This port city is located in the Netherlands and is one of the busiest ports in Europe
- It is home to Erasmus University

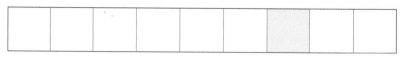

2.

- This port city can be found in British Columbia, Canada
- It has been nicknamed 'Hollywood North' due to the significant number of films that are shot in and around the city

3.

- This port city is one of the sixteen federal states of Germany
- It was once a member of the Hanseatic League

4.

- This port city is found in a small island country with a tropical climate
- The country and its capital city share the same name

5.

- This Chinese port city is located on the Yangtze river, at its estuary with the East China Sea
- It is one of the busiest ports in the world

Bonus Question:

What floating cargo was dropped from a ship in 1992, and has since been particularly helpful to oceanographers mapping out ocean currents?

CARGO SHIPPING QUIZ

At any given point in time there are around 50,000 ships on the world's oceans, transporting goods from one country to another. Around 1.8 billion tons of goods are transported by container ships every year.

Can you answer the following multiple-choice questions about international cargo shipping?

1. What percentage of all world trade is carried by sea?
   a. 75%
   b. 85%
   c. 95%

2. How many of the top ten largest container ports in the world are in China?
   a. Four
   b. Seven
   c. Eleven

3. How much greater a volume of freight is handled by Shanghai – the world's biggest container port – relative to Felixstowe, the United Kingdom's busiest container port?
   a. Five times more freight volume
   b. Ten times more freight volume
   c. Twenty times more freight volume

4. What percentage of shipping containers are made in China?
  a. 57%
  b. 77%
  c. 97%

5. Roughly how long does a container ship typically take to travel from China to the United Kingdom?
  a. One month
  b. Six weeks
  c. Two months

6. What percentage of container-ship crew members are women, internationally?
  a. 2%
  b. 8%
  c. 14%

7. How many standard shipping containers can fit onto the largest container ships?
  a. 10,000
  b. 15,000
  c. 20,000

8. Approximately how many bananas can fit into a standard 20-foot-long shipping container?
  a. 8,000
  b. 28,000
  c. 48,000

CARGO STACKING

How many cube-shaped containers can you count in each of the two arrangements opposite? Each stack began as a perfect 5 x 4 x 4 arrangement (as shown below), but some have been unloaded and taken away. There are no floating cubes.

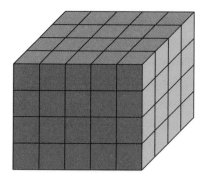

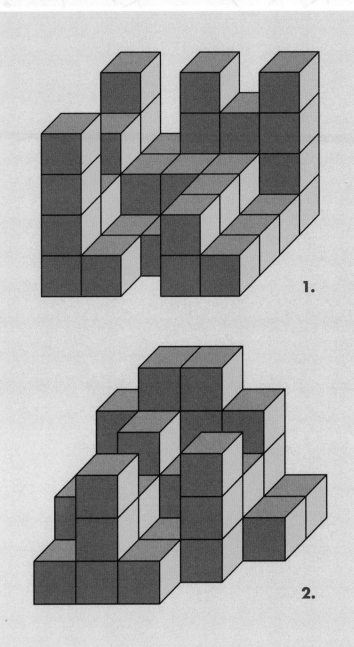

1.

2.

NAUTICAL MEASUREMENTS AND ORIENTATIONS – Ship Paths

Distances at sea are measured in nautical miles. Once calculated as 1/60th of a degree of latitude, a nautical mile was therefore historically a greater distance at the equator than at the poles, since the Earth is not a perfect sphere. Nowadays a standard distance of 6,080 feet (1,853 metres) is used.

The speed of ships is measured in knots, where one knot is equal to one nautical mile per hour.

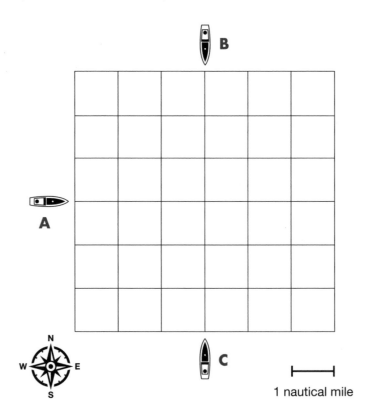

1 nautical mile

The instructions below describe the separate routes of three ships across the grid. Draw the three routes on the grid, in order to reveal a nautical shape. What does it represent?

SHIP A

- Travel south-east to a point three nautical miles south and three nautical miles east of your starting point.
- Turn ninety degrees to port and travel until you are three nautical miles further east.

SHIP B

- Travel south at fifteen knots for six minutes.
- Drop your speed to ten knots, and travel east for a further six minutes.

SHIP C

- Travel in a northerly direction for 27,360 feet.
- Turn ninety degrees to port and travel for 6,080 feet.

HIDDEN ROUTES

A ship has travelled along a route from grid square A to grid square B. Based on the clues outside the grid, can you draw in the route that the ship took? Each number specifies the exact number of grid squares in its row or column that the ship visited.

You also know that the ship never retraced its route in a way that would have involved it entering a square immediately next to one it had already visited, including diagonally touching squares, or revisited any square.

The ship only travelled in the cardinal compass directions, never moving diagonally across the grid.

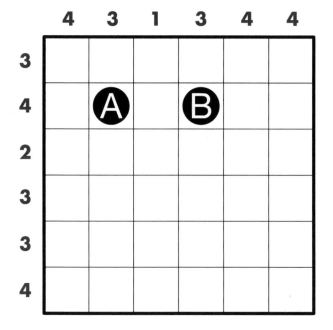

Now try this larger puzzle:

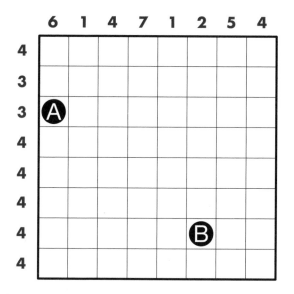

And finally try this third puzzle, where not all clues are given. In these rows and columns, the ship can visit any number of squares.

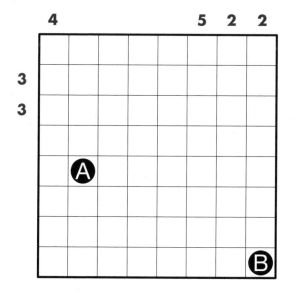

GHOST SHIPS

Over the years, legends have emerged about spectral 'ghost ships' that have been sighted at specific times, or in particular places at sea, which are often the subject of stories about sinister supernatural events. The term 'ghost ship' can also refer to real vessels that have been found drifting at sea, abandoned, giving rise to speculation about the fates of their crews.

HMS Erebus *passing through a chain of icebergs, 1842. HMS* Erebus *and its sister ship, HMS* Terror, *as well as the crew of 129 men, disappeared in the late 1840s on their ill-fated search for the Northwest Passage. The wreck was discovered on the seabed in 2014.*

HIDDEN SHIPS

Hidden on the grid below are the names of five ghost ships. You can find the ships by using the following coordinates, which it is up to you to decode:

1. E9 H11 N7 O1 I5 F2 L4
2. M6 G13 A8 L9   E4 M14 O10 B12 D7 J10 J3
3. N12 C10 G9 H9 L4 J14 K14   B6   B1 M8 N8 H3 A15 N3 D9
4. H7 J12 C5 G4 D12 K2 B3 F15
5. L12 N11 C14 M2   C2 B8 G6 O5 N9 E8 F12 D4

I	H	E	R	H	S	Q	N	H	K	A	I	P	C	V
D	S	D	B	I	O	L	F	A	L	L	R	E	Y	H
B	A	V	R	W	L	A	E	R	A	J	X	F	Z	N
N	E	A	V	D	N	F	P	L	C	R	L	J	C	W
M	C	V	R	T	I	M	Q	D	V	C	P	U	A	E
M	Z	A	E	C	B	V	M	D	T	O	I	F	L	L
I	R	T	G	S	Q	R	R	F	B	Y	Y	E	B	I
R	O	W	V	O	S	A	L	P	M	D	D	E	E	R
X	P	G	S	B	E	U	O	K	R	G	H	D	U	V
N	A	S	F	A	O	V	L	Q	P	N	O	M	A	P
C	E	T	U	L	N	E	R	N	A	V	X	M	E	I
T	B	L	D	C	T	A	E	N	P	K	O	L	R	T
C	U	I	G	W	E	D	R	R	E	B	K	U	N	L
N	E	L	P	Q	D	Q	D	I	R	I	D	Y	J	P
W	D	R	T	U	R	A	E	S	O	A	F	A	R	A

Once you have found the names of the ships, can you decide which ship is associated with each of the events described on the following pages?

A.

- The Roman Emperor Augustus shared a name with this ship.
- It is said to have been found with the crew frozen to death on board, with some in their beds and others in the act of going about their duties.
- A man was found midway through writing a diary entry that read: '11th November 1762; we have now been enclosed in the ice seventy days. The fire went out yesterday, and our master has been trying ever since to kindle it again without success. His wife died yesterday. There is no relief . . .'

B.

- The captain of this ghost ship and his wife murdered the first mate after docking near the Embarcadero in San Francisco. They then threw his headless body into the sea, keeping his head under the captain's bunk.
- Under a new captain, four crew members mutinied and killed their captain within a month.
- The ship is said to have been dismantled after multiple night-watchmen quit due to ghostly experiences of hands covered in blood gripping their sleeves, and severed heads rolling out from under the bed.

C.

- This famous ship was discovered near the Azores in 1872 with the lifeboat missing.
- The boat, cargo and items on board had been abandoned, and the fate of the crew was never discovered.

D.

- This commercial schooner was built in 1919 and named after the son of the shipbuilding company's owner.
- It was found in 1921 near Cape Hatteras in North Carolina, with no one on board.
- Some put the event down to the Bermuda Triangle.

E.

- This ship shares part of its name with a title used by certain British nobles.
- It is said to have been wrecked on Goodwin Sands in February 1748; the first mate was in love with the captain's wife and wrecked the ship in a jealous rage.
- The ship is said to reappear once every 50 years.

Bonus Question:
Which of these five ships were real and which are legendary?

GHOSTLY INITIALS

The following coordinates spell out two initials in a certain way. The initials are of a famous ghost ship, which is said to be doomed to sail the oceans forever. What is its name?

- D1 – D7 – H7 – D7 – D4 – G4 – D4 – D1
- J1 – J7 – M6 – M2 – J1

SOLUTIONS

Types of Ship – Ship Code
1. SLOOP
2. SCHOONER
3. CLIPPER
4. CUTTER
5. CARAVEL
6. FRIGATE
7. GALLEON
8. BARQUE
9. JUNK
10. GUNBOAT

1	2	3	4	5	6	7	8	9	10	11	12	13	14	15	16	17	18	19	20
K	P	A	G	U	N	R	L	B	E	O	J	S	C	F	T	H	Q	I	V

Multi-Hull Boats
In the code, H refers to a hull, SH to a small hull, O to an outrigger and B to a beam joining parts of the frame together. The numbers give the count of each:
1. Canoe (H1) – **A**
2. Single Outrigger Canoe (H1O1B2) – **E**
3. Double Outrigger Canoe (H1O2B4) – **C**
4. Drua (H1SH1B3) – **D**
5. Catamaran (H2B2) – **B**
6. Trimaran (H1SH2B4) – **F**

Shipbuilding Materials
The six materials are OAK, ELM, BEECH, FIR, HEMP and FLAX

HULL PLANKS: Oak – this is a strong, damage resistant wood that was good for building hulls

OTHER PLANKS: Elm, Beech

MAST: Fir – the flexibility of this wood was useful for masts

SAILS AND ROPE: Hemp, Flax

Shipbuilders

CARPENTER

CAULKER

JOINER

RIGGER

SAILMAKER

SHIPWRIGHT

Parts of a Ship

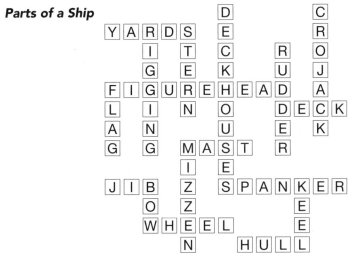

Figureheads

1. Florence Nightingale – **B**

2. William Wilberforce – **D**

3. Vice-Admiral Lord Nelson – **A**

4. President Abraham Lincoln – **C**

5. Nannie Dee (also referred to as *Cutty Sark*) – **E**

Bonus Question: the names of the ships to which the figureheads were attached are:

1. Florence Nightingale – *Florence Nightingale*
2. William Wilberforce – *William Wilberforce*
3. Vice-Admiral Lord Nelson – HMS *Horatio*
4. President Abraham Lincoln – *Abraham Lincoln*
5. Nannie Dee – *Cutty Sark*

Sails

The solution spells out 'ANY PORT IN A STORM':

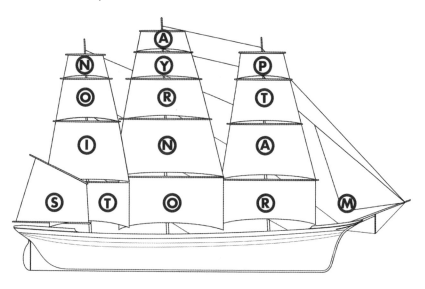

Knots

A. Bowline
B. Clove hitch
C. Double sheet bend
D. Figure of eight
E. Reef knot
F. Round turn and two half hitches

Cutty Sark Crossword

The highlighted letters spell out an anagram of AUSTRALIA, which was a frequent destination of *Cutty Sark* as part of the wool trade.

Cargo Pairs

WOOL

WINE

COAL

HOPS

SPIRITS

JUTE

CANDLES

CASTOR OIL

SARDINES

HMS *Belfast*

1. A battery. Start in the vegetable preparing space (where you might find a cabbage), then go up to the P.O.'s bathroom &

cleansing station (a place for a wash). Go up a level to the command planning room (a room where strategy meetings might take place), then across to the Admiral's bridge (an admiral is a high-ranking officer). The battery repair room E.M.R. (S) is directly beneath here, two decks below.

2. A drop in temperature. Start in the arctic store (a room where you might be able to pick up some equipment for an expedition to the North Pole) on the Forecastle Deck. Go down to the paint shop (a room where you may be able to purchase decorating supplies) and head towards the stern to the mess space that is also labelled 'clothing issue room' (a room where you can both relax and collect clothes). Go down to the flour store/B shell room/bulk clothing store (a storage room for both clothing and cooking supplies), then through the canteen store/main naval store/gunners armament store (a room where you might find a store of guns) to the cold & cool rooms, which may well be colder in temperature!

Ship Naming – Missing Vowels
The three categories are royal family members, classical mythology and English locations.

Royal Family Members
ELIZABETH
ROYAL ANNE
ROYAL GEORGE
ROYAL WILLIAM
MARY

Classical Mythology
AGAMEMNON
MINOTAUR

NEPTUNE
AJAX
MARS

English Locations
OXFORD
SUFFOLK
ESSEX
YORK
NOTTINGHAM

Ship Naming – Ship Classes

- Early 20th-Century Destroyers:
  V-Class, all beginning with the letter 'V'.
- Modern Navy Destroyers:
  Daring Class, all beginning with the letter 'D'.
- WWII Corvettes:
  Flower Class, all of these ships are named after flowers.

Early 20th-Century Destroyers
HMS *Valentine*
HMS *Valkyrie*
HMS *Valorous*
HMAS *Vampire*

Modern Navy Destroyers
HMS *Daring*
HMS *Diamond*
HMS *Dragon*
HMS *Defender*

World War II
Corvettes

HMS *Snowdrop*
HMS *Tulip*
HMS *Sunflower*
HMS *Narcissus*

Bonus Question: A bottle, often of champagne, is smashed against it.

Commercial Shipping – Hidden Port
The hidden port is DUBAI:
ROTTER**D**AM
VANCO**U**VER
HAM**B**URG
SING**A**PORE
SHANGHA**I**

Bonus Question: A large quantity of bath toys, including ducks, frogs and turtles

Cargo Shipping Quiz
1. c. 95%
2. b. Seven
3. b. Ten times more freight volume
4. c. 97%
5. a. One month
6. a. 2%
7. b. 15,000
8. c. 48,000

Cargo Stacking
1. 42 cubes
2. 38 cubes

Nautical Measurements and Orientations – Ship Paths

The three routes combine to make the shape of an anchor.

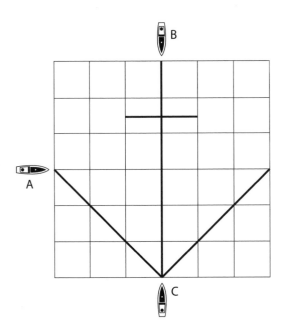

Hidden Routes

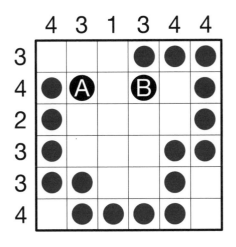

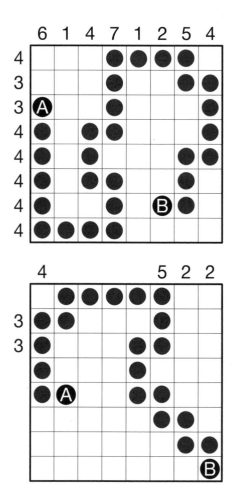

Ghost Ships – Hidden Ships

The names of the ships can be found by treating A to O as horizontal column indexes, from left to right, and 1 to 15 as vertical indexes, from bottom to top.

The names are:

1. SQUANDO
2. MARY CELESTE

3. CARROLL A DEERING

4. OCTAVIUS

5. LADY LOVIBOND

The descriptions are:

SQUANDO – **B**

MARY CELESTE – **C**

CARROLL A DEERING – **D**

OCTAVIUS – **A**

LADY LOVIBOND – **E**

Bonus Question:

The *Mary Celeste*, *Carroll A Deering* and *Squando* were all real ships. The *Octavius* and the *Lady Lovibond* are legendary.

Ghost Ships – Ghostly Initials

Join the squares indicated by the coordinates, using the same indexing as in the previous question, and you will draw the letters 'F' and 'D'. These are the initials of the *Flying Dutchman*.

CHAPTER 3

CULTURE, MYTH AND LEGEND

This chapter is based on traditions and cultural practices that have roots in seafaring, both factual and fictional. The vast human experience of life at sea has influenced language and literature, and has given rise to numerous superstitions, customs and traditions. Some readers may be familiar with these already and some may not be aware of the nautical origins. So, if you're at a loose end,* test your knowledge and observational skills in the following codewords, crosswords, pathfinders and quizzes!

* A common phrase, which stems from when sailors would tie up loose ends of rigging to ensure that a boat was shipshape.

ISLANDIA MAP

The stunning map spanning the previous two pages is entitled *Islandia*, and was drafted by Anders Vedel in 1595. It was the first printed map of Iceland, and forms part of the National Maritime Museum's vast collection of sea charts and maps, which range from the medieval period to the present day. This particular map is very geographically accurate for its time, so it is assumed that it was compiled with the help of at least one native Icelander. Other maps of the period are sometimes heavily based on hearsay.

Can you answer the following questions about the *Islandia* map?

1. One geological feature states in its Latin label that it 'throws stones' and is 'forever condemned'. Which heavily illustrated feature on the map is being described? It is still known by the same name today. You can see the stones in the image.

2. In 2010 the volcano Eyjafjallajökull erupted, spewing volcanic ash and dust into the atmosphere and making most European air travel impossible. The volcano is labelled on this map, but can you find it? The spelling is not identical to the modern place name, but it is very similar.

3. The Icelandic word 'jökull', seen in the volcano name Eyjafjallajökull in the previous question, appears prominently several times on the map in its older form of 'iokul'. Given that it does not mean 'volcano', what do you think it might mean?

4. Why do you think so many sea monsters feature on the map?

5. The cloud-like feature labelled 'O' on the map is identified on the reverse of the map as 'spermaceti', which was described as 'a base kind of amber, they commonly call Hualambur'. Produced by whales, what was this substance used for?

6. The following description is given on the reverse side for one large illustration on the map:

Huge and marvailous great heaps of ice brought hither with the tide from the frozen sea, making great and terrible noise and some pieces of which oft times are fourty cubites bigge; upon these in some places white beares do sitte closely, watching the silly fish which here about to play and sport themselves.

a. Which letter label on the map is associated with the illustration described above?
b. What is inconsistent about the written description and the image as shown on the map?

7. There is no letter label 'J' on the map. Why?

SEA-CREATURE SAFARI

Sea monsters were often included on sixteenth- and seventeenth-century maps, and the map of *Islandia* shown in the previous question is a particularly good example. Many different depictions of animals both real and fictional can be found in its waters.

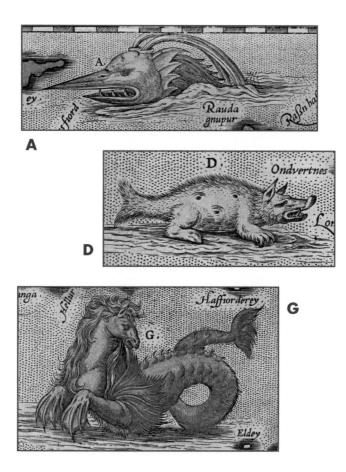

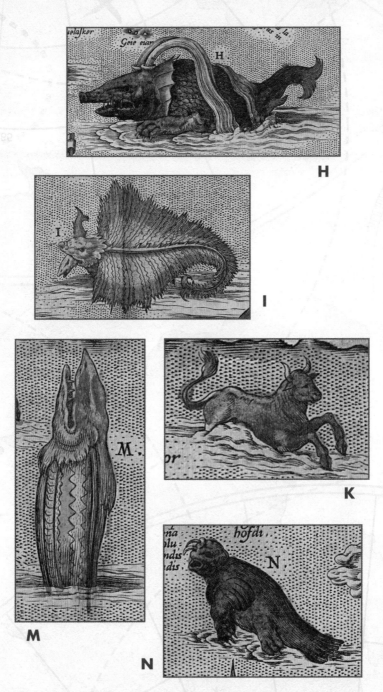

Can you match the images of sea creatures on the previous two pages with their descriptions below, taken from the reverse of the original map?

- **HROSHAULUR**, *that is as much to say the* **SEA-HORSE**, *with a mane hanging downe from his neck like an horse.*

- *The* **HYENA**, *the* **SEA HOGGE**, *a monstrous kind of fish, of which thou maiest read in the 21 booke of Olaus Magnus.*

- *Is a fish they commonly call* **NAHVAL**. *If any man eateth of this fish, he dieth presently. It hath a tooth in the forepart of his head, standing out seuen cubittes. This diuers have sold for the Unicornes horne.*

- **ROSTINGER** *(which is also called a Rosmar), is somewhat like a* **SEA-CALFE**: *it goeth to the bottom of the sea upon four feet, but very short ones. His skinne may be scarcely pierced with any weapon. Hee sleepeth twelve houres together hanging by his two long teeth upon some rock or cliffe.*

- **STAUKUL**, *the Dutchmen call it Springual; he hath beene seene to stand a whole day together upright upon his taile. It is so called of leaping and skipping.*

- **SKAUTUHVALURM**: *this fish altogether full of griffes and bones; is somewhat like a ray or skaite but an infinite deal bigger: when it appeareth it is like an island, and with his finnes overturns shippes and boates.*

- **SEENAUT, SEA COWES,** of colour gray: they sometimes come out of the sea and do feed upon the land, many in company together. They have a little bagge hanging at their nose, by the help of which they live in the water.

- The greatest kind of **WHALES**, which seldome sheweth itselfe; it is more like a little island, than a fish. It cannot follow or chase the smaller fishes, by reason of the huge greatnesse and weight of his body.

Bonus Question:

Which one of these animals is now known as a walrus?

LEGENDARY LOCATIONS

Can you answer these questions about eight mythical maritime locations? Confirm your answers – or work them out – by deleting one letter from each of the pairs given beneath every question.

1. Whose locker, at the bottom of the ocean, are sailors said to be sent to when they die?

MD AE RV BY   JC OW NE ES ' ST

2. Which folkloric afterlife is said to be where sailors can enjoy music, mirth and dancing that never ceases?

HF EI DA DF LI FE AR ' DS   RG RO AE EH TN

3. Which famous lost island, mentioned by Plato, was supposedly submerged beneath the ocean?

LA TE LM AR BN WT IF SN

4. What is the name given to the region of the Atlantic Ocean where ships and aircraft are reported to have disappeared under mysterious circumstances?

FB EO TR RM EU DN LA   ST QR AI UA TN GD NL LE

5. What optical phenomenon is a type of mirage that can appear to show ships or floating cities above the horizon?

LF OA TW EA   MA OR CR EG RA WN AD

6. What is the name of the fabled Breton city swallowed by the sea after its sluice gates were erroneously opened?

MK AE RT - FI SN

7. Which Irish monk undertook a legendary voyage around the north Atlantic, encountering gryphons, whales and volcanoes? An island named after him appeared on several early maps of the Atlantic.

AS LT   AB NR ED NE DY RA EN

8. In Arthurian legend, what is the name given to the island of plenty where the sword Excalibur was supposedly forged?

AE RV GA LT AO NS

Locker at the bottom of the ocean, by William Lionel Wyllie.

MYTHICAL MONSTERS CROSSWORD

Sea monster illustrations, from Twenty Thousand Leagues
Under the Sea, *a science-fiction adventure novel by*
Jules Verne, first published in 1870.

Can you complete the crossword opposite, where all of the solutions
are the names of mythical beasts or beings? Once complete, the
letters in the highlighted squares will reveal a name shared by
two entirely separate prominent characters in nautical fiction. The
letters will need to be rearranged to reveal the hidden name.

ACROSS

5 Tentacled Greek monster stationed opposite 4-down (6)

7 Enchanting songstresses who lure sailors to their deaths (6)

8 Constellation and monster that gives modern whales and dolphins their scientific name (5)

9 Many-headed serpent slain by Hercules (5)

10 Biblical monster, also used to refer generally to large sea creatures (9)

DOWN

1 Sign of the Zodiac and water-dwelling goat (9)

2 Legendary cephalopod of huge size (6)

3 Nickname of Scottish loch-dwelling beast (6)

4 Monster from Greek legend, depicted as a whirlpool (9)

6 Giant water serpent believed to dwell in the Amazon (8)

GODS AND GODDESSES OF THE SEA

Reveal the names of six different major sea gods and goddesses by cracking the number code, in which each letter has been replaced by a number. The mythology to which each god or goddess belongs is also given. A grid is provided for you to keep track of your deductions, and three letters are already solved to get you started.

Letters to use: **A D E I L M N O P R S T U V Y**

Irish

1	13	10 R

Welsh

1	1	15	10 R

Greek

2	12	7	14	13	3	12	5

Roman

5	14	2	11	9	5	14

Inuit

7	14	3	5	4

Finnish

8 V	14	1	1	4	6 M	12

1	2	3	4	5	6	7	8	9	10	11	12	13	14	15
					M		V		R					

GREEK SEA GODS WORD SEARCH

Greek mythology has many different deities connected with the sea, from major gods and beasts through to water nymphs and mermaids. Can you find the names of some of these divine beings hidden in the word search below? A list of the names to find has been provided on the opposite page.

```
I  C  H  T  H  Y  E  S  L  L  G  R  G  E  E
C  P  F  Y  G  N  U  B  T  H  A  U  M  A  S
H  R  A  V  E  N  L  A  M  I  A  Y  E  A  S
T  G  U  L  I  D  O  R  I  S  C  A  R  E  G
H  X  A  C  L  Z  G  A  K  I  R  T  T  N  O
Y  G  R  J  B  A  A  N  S  G  C  I  I  S  C
O  A  P  T  S  K  S  E  Q  E  R  H  U  A  E
C  E  B  O  L  A  H  R  L  E  P  E  E  P  A
E  R  O  J  N  T  F  E  N  L  R  T  Q  R  N
N  H  A  L  N  T  E  I  E  E  A  O  M  O  U
T  A  E  E  Y  D  U  D  N  L  C  I  T  T  S
A  L  B  L  O  C  F  S  A  F  Z  I  V  E  I
U  I  J  H  L  L  A  G  M  Q  R  N  O  U  S
R  A  R  D  L  E  U  C  O  T  H  E  A  S  Z
S  E  C  A  L  L  I  S  T  E  L  A  D  O  N
```

AEOLUS	GRAEAE	NERITES
BENTHESICYME	HALIAE	OCEANUS
CALLISTE	HELLE	OEOLYCA
CARCINUS	ICHTHYES	PALLAS
DELPHIN	ICHTHYOCENTAURS	PONTUS
DORIS	LADON	PROTEUS
ELECTRA	LAMIA	RHODE
EROTES	LEUCOTHEA	THAUMAS
GALATEA	NEREIDS	THOOSA
GALENE	NEREUS	TRITON

Now see if you can identify the following gods, goddesses and deities that all featured in the wordsearch:

1. The commander of dolphins, who has a constellation named after him

2. They can be seen in the seen in the sky as a constellation and fourth Zodiac sign

3. The merman son of Poseidon and Amphitrite, often pictured carrying a conch shell

4. She gives her name to the stretch of water swum across by the legendary hero Leander

5. A band of fifty sea nymphs famed for their kindness towards sailors

PIRATE PATHFINDER

A colour plate taken from P. Christian's Histoire Des Pirates
et Corsaires, *published in 1852, depicting British sailors
boarding an Algerine pirate ship.*

The image of the pirate is one that has never failed to capture the
imagination, forming the subject of literature, theatre and film for
centuries. Though pirates have existed since ancient times, the golden
age of piracy was in the seventeenth and early eighteenth centuries.
During this time more than 5,000 pirates were said to be at sea.

Hidden in the grid opposite are the names of five historical
pirates. Reveal their names by drawing a continuous path that visits
each square exactly once and never crosses itself, spelling out the
names as it goes. The path can travel horizontally and vertically
between touching letters, but never diagonally.

To help you, clues about the identity of the pirates are given on
the opposite page, with the number of letters in each name given
in brackets. The names in the grid are found in the same order as
the clues given opposite.

Your path should start at the 'in' arrow and end at the 'out' arrow.

a. A pirate-hunter turned pirate, best known for reportedly burying his treasure (7, 4)

b. A notoriously barbaric pirate better known by the alias 'Blackbeard' (6, 5)

c. A Welsh pirate whose short career was one of the most successful of the 'Golden Age of Piracy' (11, 7)

d. A female pirate who was married to two Irish chieftains, and was eventually pardoned by Elizabeth I (5, 7)

e. A Chinese pirate who commanded a fleet of around 800 junks after her husband's death (5, 3, 4)

↓

T	R	A	E	T	I	L	W
H	A	C	R	D	A	L	I
O	B	H	A	W	M	K	I
L	O	M	E	D	E	D	D
B	O	R	W	A	L	Y	C
E	R	E	O	M	L	E	H
S	T	C	I	Y	G	N	I
G	R	A	H	S	A	O	U

→

MARY READ AND ANNE BONNY

*Mary Read (left) and Anne Bonny (right), two of the
most infamous female pirates in history.*

While reliable accounts of female pirates are few and far between,
two women became notable during the 'Golden Age of Piracy'
in the seventeenth and eighteenth centuries: Anne Bonny and
Mary Read.

Not all of the following statements about the two women are true. Can you guess which are the four false claims?

A. Anne Bonny was born in what is now Virginia in the USA

B. Anne was first married to a pirate who became an informer, contributing to the arrests of several other pirates

C. Mary Read had served as a soldier in Flanders, while dressed as a man

D. The two women, after meeting in the Caribbean, joined forces and captured a ship belonging to John Rackham, or 'Calico Jack'

E. Mary and Anne fooled the pirate crew – apart from Calico Jack – into thinking that they were men

F. Anne travelled to Cuba to give birth to Calico Jack's son

G. The women acquired matching tattoos of swallows on their arms

H. Calico Jack's ship was named *Prevarication*

I. The women and their crew were captured and tried for piracy

J. The women were tried together, and were both condemned to death

K. Both women were pregnant at the time of their trial, which granted them both a stay of execution

PIRATE FLAGS

The skull and crossbones is perhaps the most recognisable symbol of pirates on the high seas, but pirate flags incorporated many different signs and symbols into their design – mostly intended to strike fear into their victims. While it is the black flag that is most commonly associated with pirates today, the red flag is of greater antiquity and was as widespread during the great age of piracy.

The following questions are based on the various pirate flags shown opposite.

1. What nickname is given to the skull and crossbones, as shown on the flag labelled '19th century' opposite?

2. What background colour of flag, seen in the image opposite, is the traditional signifier of defiance and readiness in battle?

3. How many hourglasses can you find in total on the flags opposite, and what do you think they symbolise?

4. One of the flags opposite is often attributed to Blackbeard, who had a reputation as a particularly fearsome pirate. His flag hints at a particularly unpleasant form of death – so which flag do you think this is?

5. The Welsh pirate Bartholomew Roberts sought vengeance on the authorities of Barbados and Martinique, whose repeated attempts to capture him caused him many problems. How is this shown in one of his flag designs, opposite?

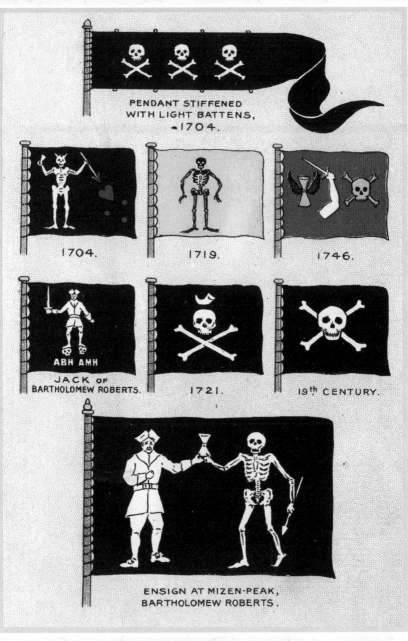

PENDANT STIFFENED
WITH LIGHT BATTENS,
-1704.

1704.

1719.

1746.

ABH AMH
JACK OF
BARTHOLOMEW ROBERTS.

1721.

19th CENTURY.

ENSIGN AT MIZEN-PEAK,
BARTHOLOMEW ROBERTS.

A selection of pirate flags and ensigns.

BURIED TREASURE

Very few pirates buried their treasure, despite many works of fiction that might lead you to think otherwise. In the grid below, however, you *do* know that several treasure chests have been hidden. Can you locate them all?

1	1			2
2		2	2	
	3	2		1
3		4		1
				1

Treasure chests are hidden in some blank squares, with no more than one chest per square. Numeric clues reveal the total number of treasure chests that can be found in touching squares, including diagonally touching squares.

Once you have found the treasure in the previous puzzle, try this trickier puzzle:

	1			2	1	
2					4	
		3	2	3		1
1	2				3	
1	3	2			3	
			2			
2	4	3		1	2	2
			2			

Now you're a treasure-hunting expert, try this tougher challenge.

		1		1			3			1
3	4		1			2			3	
		2		1		4			4	
3	3	3				4		5		2
				3					3	
3	4			3			7		4	
	5		5			5			2	2
	4				4					
	4		4		4			5	3	2
	2			1		3		4		
	3				2			3	4	2
1				2			2		1	

An illustration of a pirate captain from Howard Pyle's Book of Pirates, first published in 1921 and now within the National Maritime Museum's Caird Library.

SAILOR SUPERSTITIONS

These two kittens were photographed on board HMS
Hawkins and are in the muzzle of a 7.5-inch gun.

The clues below refer to eight nautical superstitions and apparent
omens – both good and bad – which have been passed down over
the years. Can you work out what, or who, is being described in
each case?

To help you, the solutions are also given on the opposite page
– but they are out of order and have had the letters of each word
sorted into alphabetical order.

1. This might be considered a good or a bad sign – depending
on whether you see it at night, or in the morning

2. To have one of these on board was considered lucky

3. This fruit was considered very unlucky; not only does it spoil quickly, but is a perfect hiding place for poisonous spiders

4. To change this at sea would be considered very bad luck – unless a special ceremony took place to remove all of its original traces first

5. To kill one of these is considered to be extremely bad luck

6. This is a particularly unlucky day to set sail

7. To do this on a ship would be tantamount to challenging the wind itself, and risk bringing bad luck

8. You might find them on the front of a ship, or even in its name, but these were frequently considered unlucky to have on board in person

AAABNN

AABLORSST

ACT

ADFIRY

DER KSY

EHILSTW

EMNOW

HIPSS' AEMN

NAUTICAL EXPRESSIONS

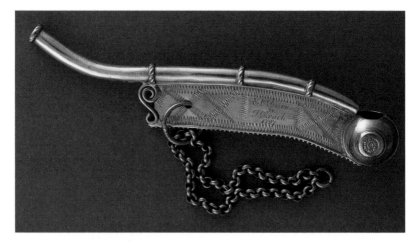

*Bosun's call by Hester Bateman, 1788, used after the Battle of
Copenhagen, 1797. The bosun's call was a pipe traditionally used
to pass commands to the crew. Its high pitch whistle meant it
could be heard over the sound of the sea and weather.*

Life on the seven seas created a unique culture, with its own idioms
and expressions. The seven phrases described opposite are now
widely used outside of a nautical context, but they have their roots
in seafaring. Can you work out which well-known idioms each of
the following descriptions refers to?

1. Used now to describe an unpredictable character, this expression would have indicated a literal threat to sailors when a piece of weaponry had broken free of its constraints

2. This expression – now used to indicate the completion of a task – comes from the practice of stitching and sealing a deceased sailor into his hammock for sea burial

3. Now an informal way to tell someone to be quiet, this phrase arose from the bosun's final call instructing sailors to settle in for the night

4. This navigational expression apparently stems from the practice of releasing birds from a ship to help sailors find land, as birds would take the most direct route there

5. This expression describes the final part of a line, chain or cable remaining on a ship when the anchor is being weighed, and now refers generally to the final part of a task

6. The practice of making a quick escape by slicing the ropes that hold you in port and not weighing anchor has given us this expression, which still means to leave hurriedly – and possibly under dubious circumstances

7. A good sailor with a solid understanding of the technicalities of sailing would be said to have this competency, which is now used generally to describe the quality of being familiar with the details of a task or practice

MARITIME MEANINGS

Naval telescope, typical of those used on board ships in the nineteenth century. The barrel panel shows signalling flags used by ships at this time.

Can you match each of these maritime words with one of the definitions below? Some decoy definitions – which don't apply to any of these words – have been added to make it trickier.

ABAFT

BINNACLE

DUNNAGE

ESCUTCHEON

SCUTTLEBUTT

THALASSOPHOBIA

VEXILLOLOGY

A. A fear of the sea, open water, or being far from land
B. A ship that has broken free of its moorings is said to be this
C. The part of a ship's stern where the name is painted or engraved
D. The red-and-white chequered flag used to signify a ship leaving port
E. A ship's store of drinking water, as well as meaning 'to gossip'
F. The study of flags
G. Loose wooden planks put down to keep cargo in position and clear of bilge water
H. The structure in which a ship's compass sits
I. A nickname for a sailor charged with running messages to the captain
J. Behind the stern; toward the back

SEA SHANTIES

*An etching by George Cruikshank, 1825, showing
a caricature of sailors carousing.*

The sea shanty is an iconic feature of maritime culture, although
the precise lyrics, structures and themes of individual shanties can
vary from place to place, and sailor to sailor. To be classed as a
'shanty', a song must have been used as a working song to get
everyone toiling together – this usually involved either pulling
something (hauling) or pushing something (heaving). Shanties
usually have easy choruses for everyone to join in with, and songs
in the 'shanty style' are still being written today.

Working shanties were never sung ashore as this would have
been considered very bad luck – the old sailors were extremely
superstitious. Additionally, some songs were used by sailors for
leisure purposes.

On the following pages you can find four abridged popular shanties. Versions of these songs might have had many more additional verses, depending on who was singing them. Then on the following pages you can find some questions about the shanties and their lyrics.

Blow the Man Down

Come all you young fellows that follows the sea
To me way, hay, blow the man down!
Now please pay attention and listen to me
Give me some time to blow the man down

I'm a deep water sailor just come from Hong Kong
If you give me some whisky, I'll sing you a song
On a trim Black Ball liner, I first served me time
On a trim Black Ball liner, I wasted me prime

Nelson's Blood/Roll the Old Chariot Along

And a drop of Nelson's blood wouldn't do us any harm,
a drop of Nelson's blood wouldn't do us any harm,
a drop of Nelson's blood wouldn't do us any harm,
and we'll all hang on behind

And, we'll roll the old chariot along,
we'll roll the old chariot along,
we'll roll the old chariot along
and we'll all hang on behind

South Australia

In South Australia I was born
(To me) heave away, haul away
In South Australia round Cape Horn
We're bound for South Australia
Haul away you rolling kings
To me heave away, haul away
Haul away, you'll hear me sing
We're bound for South Australia

Spanish Ladies

Farewell and adieu to you, Spanish Ladies
Farewell and adieu to you, ladies of Spain;
For we've received orders for to sail for old England
But we hope in a short time to see you again

We will rant and we'll roar like true British sailors
We'll rant and we'll roar all on the salt seas
Until we strike soundings in the channel of old England;
From Ushant to Scilly is thirty-five leagues

Try answering these questions on the sea shanties on the preceding pages:

1. First, locate the phrases in the lyrics of the sea shanties that match the following descriptions:

    a. A reference to rum, which was once rationed to sailors in the Royal Navy

    b. A reference to the accidental knocking-down of a ship by a sudden gust of wind

    c. A traditionally treacherous part of a circumnavigator's route

    d. A unit of measurement for distance, usually on land

    e. An instruction for users of a capstan, which was used for bringing in ropes and sails

    f. The name of a packet-ship company travelling between Liverpool and New York City

2. Each of the shanties has further verses. Can you guess which shanty each of these lines from a later verse belongs to?

    a. *Oh a plate of Irish stew wouldn't do us any harm*

    b. *There ain't but one thing grieves my mind*

    c. *We'll drink and be jolly and drown melancholy*

    d. *As I walked out one morning fair*

    e. *It's starboard and larboard on deck you will sprawl*

THE SEA IN LITERATURE

Medal commemorating R. L. Stevenson's novel Treasure Island.

Can you work out which novel, play or epic poem is being described by each of the following entries? All of the works have nautical themes.

The titles of each work are also given, out of order, on the opposite page – but their letters have been jumbled up. Note that the spaces and punctuation in the jumbled titles do not necessarily correspond with those in the original title.

Can you match each description to the correct unjumbled title?

1.   This epic poetic ballad is most famous for its inclusion of an albatross shot by the protagonist, which brings about ill fortune for the crew on board his ship

2.   This play takes place largely on an island, where a ship has been wrecked following a violent storm brought about by supernatural forces

3. This epic poem tells of a hero's ten-year journey home from the Trojan war, beset by trials and the wrath of deities

4. In this fairy tale a young sea-dwelling girl exchanges her voice for a human body and soul

5. This novel details one seafarer's quest for revenge on the white whale that severed his leg on a previous voyage

6. This short novel explores the fortunes of an ageing fisherman in Cuba, as he attempts to catch a giant marlin

7. This science-fiction novel with a nautical distance in the title follows the adventures of an enigmatic captain aboard his submarine-like vessel, journeying through real and fictional areas of the ocean depths

8. This adventure novel is perhaps most famous for its inclusion of the fictional pirate Long John Silver – as well as several real pirates – and follows one boy and a ship on a quest for buried treasure

SHY EYE DOTS

UNREAL DISASTER

I'M BY DOCK

HUGE WATER AS UNDAUNTED, STEEL HONESTY

THE PETS MET

THE FANATIC HEROINE MERRIMENT

THE MILD ALTIMETER

HOTHEAD MAN ENDS TALE

FICTIONAL SHIPS

The letters in the names of six fictional ships from nautical literature have been jumbled below. Additionally, one extra letter has been added to each of them which, when they are extracted and read in order from top to bottom, will spell out a maritime word.

Can you extract the letters to solve the anagrams and reveal the fictional ships? Ignore the spaces when solving these anagrams – all of the ships have single-word names.

To help you, each anagram also includes a clue to reveal the type of artistic work the fictional ship first appeared in. Ship name prefixes, such as HMS, have been removed.

FINER SOAP
Opera

OPAQUED
Novel

A HIP LIAISON
Novel

A NULL SUIT
Novel

GO OAR
Epic poem

RED POISON
Novel

WORD JOURNEYS

Can you voyage from the start to the end of each of these word-based journeys? Simply change one letter per step to create a regular four-letter word, without rearranging any letters. The first has been completed as an example.

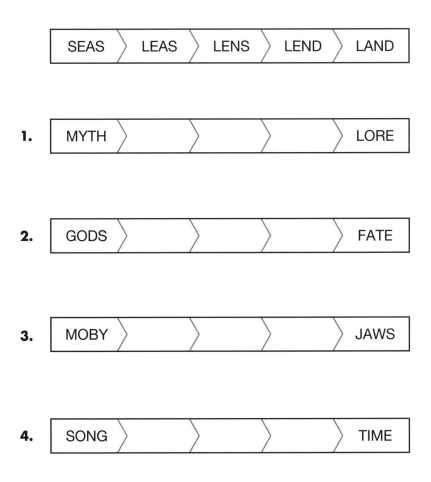

| SEAS | LEAS | LENS | LEND | LAND |

1. | MYTH | | | | LORE |

2. | GODS | | | | FATE |

3. | MOBY | | | | JAWS |

4. | SONG | | | | TIME |

CODED SEA QUOTES

Seascape by marine artist William Lionel Wyllie, c.1890.

Crack the codes to reveal six quotes about the sea. Each quote has been encoded using a simple alphabet-shift cipher, in which each letter has been shifted forward a fixed number of positions in the alphabet. Shifts past the end of the alphabet continue again from A. For example, LIGHTHOUSE with each letter shifted forward by two would become NKIJVJQWUG.

Each quote uses a different shift. Can you work out the size of shift used for each, and therefore restore the original quotes and their attributions?

1. Wkh vhd, rqfh lw fdvwv lwv vshoo, krogv rqh
   lq lwv qhw ri zrqghu iruhyhu

   – Mdftxhv-Byhv Frxvwhdx

2. Xs qi xli wie mw e gsrxmryep qmvegpi

   – Aepx Almxqer

3. Ymj xjf nx jajwdymnsl

   – Ozqjx Ajwsj

4. Bpm dwqkm wn bpm ami axmisa bw bpm awct

   – Sibm Kpwxqv

5. Lux cngzkbkx ck ruyk (roqk g eua ux g sk),
   oz'y grcgey uax ykrl ck lotj ot znk ykg

   – K.K. lassotmy

6. Kdc vxan fxwmnaodu cqjw cqn uxan xo xum
   vnw jwm cqn uxan xo kxxtb rb cqn bnlanc
   uxan xo xlnjw

   – Q.Y. Uxenlajoc

SCRAMBLED SEA QUOTES

Can you reveal these quotes from nautical literature? Each has been concealed by reordering its words into alphabetical order, and changing capital letters to lower case. The source of each quote is given.

1. are dreams ever hands have made nearest ships that the thing to
(from *My Ship O'Dreams* by Robert N. Rose)

2. a always any be can is man new sailor sane that the wonder
(from *English Traits* by Ralph Waldo Emerson)

3. ago as five great it of on rolled rolled sea shroud the the thousand years
(from *Moby-Dick or, The Whale* by Herman Melville)

4. better drown drowned duffers duffers if not than won't
(from *Swallows and Amazons*, by Arthur Ransome)

5. a active crowded for in manned most of place service ship the the war was world
(from *Lieutenant Hornblower*, by C.S. Forester)

Illustration from Herman Melville's Moby-Dick or, The Whale.

SOLUTIONS

Islandia Map

1. Hekla. It is a large volcano depicted towards the centre of the main island of Iceland.

2. The volcano can be found just south of Hekla. On the map it is written as 'Eyafialla Iokul'.

3. *Jökull* (or 'iokul' on this map) means 'glacier' in Icelandic. Currently around 11% of Iceland is beneath glaciers.

4. Sea monsters were included on sixteenth-century and seventeenth-century maps to enchant readers, and to educate them about what could be found in the sea.

5. Up to around 2,000 litres of spermaceti could be extracted from a sperm whale, and it was heavily used for candles. It was also a base in many cosmetics and ointments, plus was also used as a lubricant and for leatherworking. The original definition of 'candlepower', a UK measurement of the intensity of light, was defined in terms of a pure spermaceti candle.

6.

a. Q, at the top-right of the map:

b. The bears are shown in the image as being brown, but are described in the accompanying text as being white. The colouring may have been added after the map was first made, however, since other versions of the same map show different colouring.

7. In texts of this era the letter 'i' was used to denote both the vowel 'i' and the consonant 'j', as well as any other sounds denoted by both letters in modern usage. You can also see this in the spelling of some words on the map, such as 'iokul' versus 'jökull' (see question 3). On this map, the letter V is also used instead of U when text is in upper case.

Sea-creature Safari

The animals associated with each label are:

- A: The Nahval
- D: The Hyena / sea hogge
- G: The Hroshaulur / Sea-horse
- H: The Whales
- I: The Skautuhvalurm
- K: The Seenaut / sea cowes
- M: The Staukul
- N: The Rostinger

Bonus Question: The Rostinger, labelled N on the original map, is believed to be a representation of the modern walrus

Legendary Locations

1. Davy Jones's
2. Fiddler's Green
3. Atlantis
4. Bermuda Triangle
5. Fata Morgana
6. Kêr-Is
7. St Brendan
8. Avalon

Mythical Monsters Crossword

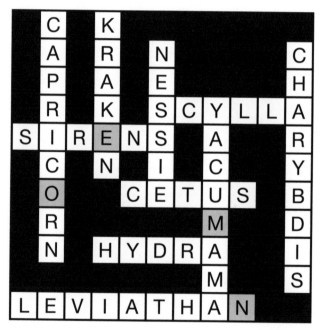

The highlighted squares can be anagrammed to spell out NEMO. Captain Nemo is found in the novel *Twenty Thousand Leagues Under the Sea*, and Nemo is (probably as a reference to the novel) also the name of the fishy protagonist in the animated film *Finding Nemo*.

Gods and Goddesses of the Sea

Irish: **LIR**
Welsh: **LLYR**
Greek: **POSEIDON**
Roman: **NEPTUNE**
Inuit: **SEDNA**
Finnish: **VELLAMO**

1	2	3	4	5	6	7	8	9	10	11	12	13	14	15
L	P	D	A	N	M	S	V	U	R	T	O	I	E	Y

Greek Sea Gods

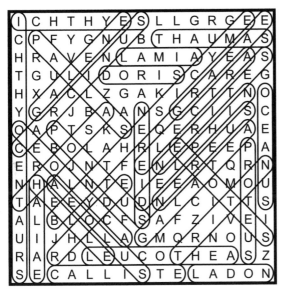

1. **Delphin** – the constellation is Delphinus
2. **Carcinus**
3. **Triton**
4. **Helle** – the stretch of water was known as the Hellespont (now Dardanelles)
5. **Nereids**

Pirate Pathfinder

a. WILLIAM KIDD
b. EDWARD TEACH
c. BARTHOLOMEW ROBERTS
d. GRACE O'MALLEY
e. CHING YIH SAOU

Mary Read and Anne Bonny

A. False. Anne was born in Ireland, and her family later moved to what is now North Carolina.

B. True

C. True

D. False. Anne and Calico Jack met in port, began an affair, and escaped to sea together. Mary joined the pair – and the crew – later.

E. True

F. True

G. False

H. False

I. True. The crew were eventually captured and put on trial in 1720.

J. True. The whole crew was tried, and sentenced to death.

K. True. The rest of the crew were executed, however, including Calico Jack.

Pirate Flags

1. (The) Jolly Roger.

2. Red. A red flag was used by pirates and non-pirates alike to demonstrate impending engagement in battle. Red flags are still used today as warning symbols, and the phrase 'a red flag' is used to describe a concerning situation.

3. Three hourglasses are shown in total – one on the flag labelled 1704, one on the flag labelled 1746, and one on the larger flag at the bottom of the page. They were used by pirates to imply that 'time was running out' for their enemies, and the addition of wings on the 1746 flag gives an impression of time flying away.

4. The 1704 flag, with its heart dripping blood that is said to warn of a slow and painful demise. The skeleton shown on the flag also has horns, a depiction of the devil.

5. The 'Jack of Bartholomew Roberts' flag depicts the captain standing on two skulls with the initials 'ABH' and 'AMH' written beneath. The initials represent the phrases 'A Barbadian's Head' and 'A Martinican's Head' respectively.

Buried Treasure

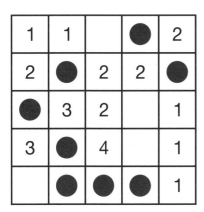

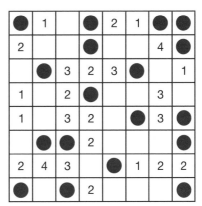

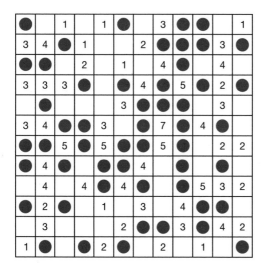

Sailor Superstitions

1. RED SKY (DER KSY)
2. CAT (ACT)
3. BANANA (AAABNN)
4. SHIP'S NAME (HIPSS' AEMN)
5. ALBATROSS (AABLORSST)
6. FRIDAY (ADFIRY)
7. WHISTLE (EHILSTW)
8. WOMEN (EMNOW)

Nautical Expressions

1. Loose cannon
2. All sewn up
3. Pipe down
4. As the crow flies
5. The bitter end
6. Cut and run
7. Knowing the ropes

Maritime Meanings

ABAFT – **J**

BINNACLE – **H**

DUNNAGE – **G**

ESCUTCHEON – **C**

SCUTTLEBUTT – **E**

THALASSOPHOBIA – **A**

VEXILLOLOGY – **F**

B, **D** and **I** therefore remain unused.

Sea Shanties

1.

a. 'Nelson's Blood'. Rum supposedly became known as this after Lord Nelson's death, when his body was stored in a spirit barrel to preserve it on the way home.

b. 'Blow the man down'. While it may refer to the knocking out of someone in a fist fight, it is thought that this refers to the moment a ship becomes half-capsized in gusty weather.

c. 'Cape Horn'. Before the creation of the Panama Canal, sailors would travel around the treacherous bottom of South America, of which Cape Horn is the southernmost mainland.

d. '(Thirty-five) leagues'. While a league is a measurement for land distances, perhaps its most famous usage is from the title of the adventure novel *Twenty Thousand Leagues Under the Sea*.

e. 'Heave away, haul away'. It is thought the song 'South Australia' might have been developed to accompany the working conditions of hauling in the anchor before a long journey.

f. 'Black Ball'. One of two liner companies of the same name, this company is also mentioned in other sea shanties. Both operated from Liverpool – one transatlantic to New York, the other to Australia.

2.

a. 'Nelson's Blood'
b. 'South Australia'
c. 'Spanish Ladies'
d. 'South Australia'
e. 'Blow the Man Down'

The Sea in Literature

1. *The Rime of the Ancient Mariner* – THE FANATIC HEROINE MERRIMENT
2. *The Tempest* – THE PETS MET
3. *The Odyssey* – SHY EYE DOTS
4. *The Little Mermaid* – THE MILD ALTIMETER
5. *Moby Dick* – I'M BY DOCK
6. *The Old Man and the Sea* – HOTHEAD MAN ENDS TALE
7. *Twenty Thousand Leagues Under the Sea* – HUGE WATER AS UNDAUNTED, STEEL HONESTY
8. *Treasure Island* – UNREAL DISASTER

Fictional Ships

PINAFORE + S – HMS *Pinafore*, from the Gilbert & Sullivan comic opera of the same name
PEQUOD + A – from Herman Melville's *Moby Dick*
HISPANIOLA + I – from Robert Louis Stephenson's *Treasure Island*
NAUTILUS + L – the submarine from Jules Verne's novels, including *Twenty Thousand Leagues Under the Sea*
ARGO + O – from Greek mythology, such as the *Argonautica*
POSEIDON + R (SS *Poseidon*) – from *The Poseidon Adventure* by Paul Gallico
The extra letters spell out SAILOR.

Word Journeys

Possible solutions are:

1. MYTH – MOTH – MOTE – MORE – LORE
2. GODS – GADS – FADS – FATS – FATE
3. MOBY – MOBS – JOBS – JABS – JAWS
4. SONG – TONG – TONE – TOME – TIME

Coded Sea Quotes

1. The sea, once it casts its spell, holds one in its net of wonder forever
   – Jacques-Yves Cousteau (shift: 3)
2. To me the sea is a continual miracle
   – Walt Whitman (shift: 4)
3. The sea is everything
   – Jules Verne (shift: 5)
4. The voice of the sea speaks to the soul
   – Kate Chopin (shift: 8)
5. For whatever we lose (like a you or a me), it's always our self we find in the sea
   – E.E. Cummings (shift: 6)
6. But more wonderful than the lore of old men and the lore of books is the secret lore of ocean
   – H.P. Lovecraft (shift: 9)

Scrambled Sea Quotes

1. Ships are the nearest thing to dreams that hands have ever made
2. The wonder is always new that any sane man can be a sailor
3. The great shroud of the sea rolled on as it rolled five thousand years ago
4. Better drowned than duffers; if not duffers won't drown
5. A ship of war manned for active service was the most crowded place in the world

CHAPTER 4

PEOPLE AND PLANS

Britain is a nation of seafarers. Life at sea has played a vital role in our heritage and national identity and the puzzles in this chapter are inspired by the key individuals, voyages and achievements of people who have lived and worked on the open ocean. Cross the globe with these daring men and women and find out about battles fought, the journeys made, the introduction of trade routes, and the exotic goods and treats that were brought to the UK by sea, which we now take for granted on our supermarket shelves.

HISTORY MAKERS AND RECORD BREAKERS

Human identity has been shaped by a relationship with the sea for centuries. Key events and personalities of the sixteenth and seventeenth centuries brought compelling stories of exploration, encounter, adventure, power, wealth and conflict. These stories paved the way for numerous achievements in the maritime world throughout history.

HMS Resolution in a gale, painted by Willem van de Velde, the Younger.

Based on your knowledge of history, can you assign each of the following feats of navigation to one of the years marked on the timeline?

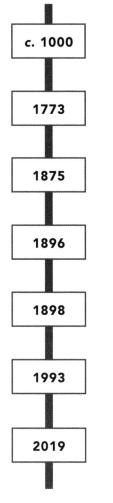

c. 1000

1773

1875

1896

1898

1993

2019

Ann Bancroft becomes the first woman to have visited both the North and South Poles

Frank Samuelson and George Harbo are the first to row across the Atlantic, doing so in 55 days

James Cook's ship the *Resolution* is the first known ship to cross the Antarctic Circle

Joshua Slocum completes the first solo circumnavigation of the world

Leifur Eiríksson lands at Vinland – the first known voyage from Europe to mainland North America

Matthew Webb completes the first known unaided swim across the English Channel

Victor Vescovo is the first person to dive to Challenger Deep – the deepest part of the World Ocean

MARITIME WOMEN

Hand-coloured lithograph by artist T.L. Leitch, showing the heroic rescue of the surviving passengers and crew of the Forfarshire *steamboat in September 1838.*

Reveal the names of five notable nautical women by cracking the number code, in which each letter has been replaced by a number. A clue to each person is provided, along with a grid to keep track of your deductions. Three letters are ready-solved to get you started.

Letters to use: **A C D E G H I L M N P R S T W Y**

1	2	3	4	5	6	7	8	9	10	11	12	13	14	15	16
M					D									H	

1. This New Englander was at one point the highest-paid lighthouse keeper in the USA, and the Lime Rock Lighthouse that she kept has since been renamed to honour her.

4	6	5
	D	

7	11	13	4	8

2. This daughter of an English lighthouse keeper is famed for her part in the rescue of sailors off the Northumberland coast in 1838.

16	2	5	14	11

6	5	2	7	4	9	16
D						

3. Born in 1723, this English woman joined the marines while dressed in male clothing, and travelled with them to India.

15	5	9	9	5	15
H					H

8	9	11	7	7

4. This English woman – under male guise – was most likely the first woman to take the shipwright's exam; she later drew a pension from the Navy under her real name, the first woman to do so.

1	5	2	3
M			

7	5	14	3

5. This American took over the command of her husband's merchant vessel when he fell ill around Cape Horn, captaining the ship to its safe return in San Francisco. At the time she was nineteen years old and pregnant with their first child.

1	5	2	3
M			

10	5	12	12	11	9

LORD HORATIO NELSON

Rear-Admiral Sir Horatio Nelson, 1758–1805,
painted by Lemuel Francis Abbott, c.1798.

Lord Horatio Nelson (29 September 1758 – 21 October 1805)
was a British naval leader who gained fame through his victories
against France and Spain during the Napoleonic Wars. His tactical
decisions brought him many successes, including the Battle of
Trafalgar – during which he died on board HMS *Victory*.

NELSON CROSSWORD

Can you complete this crossword where most of the clues relate to
Nelson's life and career?

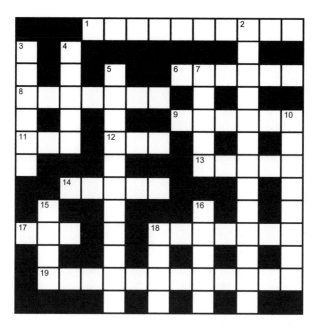

ACROSS

1 1801 naval battle in which Nelson took part; capital of Denmark (10)

6 Religious position held by Nelson's father (6)

8 Island off the west coast of Italy that Nelson helped seize in 1794 (7)

9 South London borough where Nelson lived from 1801 until his death (6)

11 Very cold; characteristic of the sea in 3-down (3)

12 Part of Nelson's body that was injured in 1794 by cannon grit (3)

13 ____shooter – a marksman, one of whom wounded Nelson during the Battle of Trafalgar (5)

14 Spanish port near the site of the Battle of Trafalgar (5)

17 Point (e.g., a cannon) at a target (3)

18 HMS _____, a Royal Navy 1940s flower-class corvette; a plant related to the buttercup (7)

19 Nelson's lover, muse of George Romney (4, 8)

DOWN

2 Coastal Norfolk town near to Nelson's birthplace (5, 8)

3 Chilly destination of one of Nelson's first sea voyages (6)

4 Captain who was the subject of Nelson's reported last words (5)

5 Nelson's rank at the time of the Battle of Trafalgar (4, 7)

7 Ridges found at sea made of rock, sand or coral (5)

10 French military leader and adversary of Nelson (8)

15 Battle of the _____, a great success for Nelson in 1798 (4)

16 Caribbean island where Nelson married Frances Nisbet (5)

18 HMS ____, a ship that took part in the Battle of Trafalgar; mythological Greek hero (4)

NELSON QUIZ

Engraving by Benjamin West and James Heath, showing the moment Nelson was struck by a musket ball fired from the French Redoutable on 21 October 1805.

1. How old was Nelson when he took his first sea voyage?
a. 10 years old
b. 12 years old
c. 15 years old

2. At which London landmark is Nelson buried?
a. Westminster Abbey
b. Southwark Cathedral
c. St Paul's Cathedral

3. At what age did Nelson first become a captain?
   a. 20
   b. 24
   c. 27

4. How many orders of knighthood did Nelson have by the time he died?
   a. 2
   b. 4
   c. 6

5. Which animal was Nelson reported to have battled with on an early voyage?
   a. A snake
   b. A moose
   c. A polar bear

6. Nelson's coffin was a gift from his fellow officer Captain Benjamin Hallowell. What was it made from?
   a. The mast of L'Orient, a French ship devastated at the Battle of the Nile
   b. Wood from the interior of his cabin on the HMS Victory
   c. The frame from his bed

THE BATTLE OF TRAFALGAR

The Battle of Trafalgar is one of the most famous naval battles in British history. The battle plan shown here indicates Nelson's tactics. Two British squadrons, commanded by Nelson and Collingwood, split the French and Spanish line, taking the fight directly to the enemy and ultimately giving the British the advantage, despite having fewer ships.

This image shows a plan of the Battle of Trafalgar, giving the position of various ships. Use the key to find each of the ships listed below and trace a series of paths between them on the battle plan, in the order given, to reveal the surname of the signal officer who was on board the *Victory* during the battle. Each path spells out one letter of his name.

1. Corneille – Pickle – Africa – Scipio – M. Blanc

2. Boheme – Monarco – Argus – L'Aigle – Swiftsure

3. Dreadnought – Defiance – Fougueux – Sovereign – Rhin – Swiftsure

4. Indomitable – Belleisle – Thémise – Argus

5. Trinidada – Cutter – St. Augustin – Furet – Trinidada

PLAN OF THE BATTLE OF TRAFALGAR.

THE BATTLE OF TRAFALGAR—NAMES OF VESSELS ENGAGED.

	GUNS.			GUNS.			GUNS.
1. Spartiate,	74	26. Polyphemus,	74	51. El Royet	100
2. Minotaur,	74	27. Achille,	74	52. Bel Asile.	
3. Orion,	74	28. Bellerophon,	74	53. St. Juan,	74
4. Ajax,	74	29. Mars,	74	54. Algesiras,	74
5. Agamemnon,	64	30. Belleisle,	74	55. Argonaut,	80
6. Conqueror,	74	31. Sovereign,	100	56. Swiftsure,	74
7. Leviathan,	74	32. Argonaut,	74	57. Argonaut,	74
8. Britannia,	100	33. Hermione, f.		58. Ildefonso,	74
9. Neptune,	98	34. Intrepide,	74	59. Pr. d'Asturias,	112
10. Téméraire,	98	35. Pluto,	74	60. L'Aigle,	74
11. Victory,	100	36. Fougueux,	74	61. Rhin, f.	
12. Cutter.		37. Monarco,	74	62. Montara,	74
13. Naide, f.		38. St. Anna,	112	63. Berwick,	74
14. Phœbe, f.		39. Indomitable,	84	64. Achillo,	74
15. Sirius, f.		40. Leander,	64	65. Boheme,	74
16. Africa,	64	41. Redoubtable,	74	66. Thémise, f.	
17. Pickle, sch.		42. Bucentaur,	80	67. Argus.	
18. Euryalus, f.		43. Trinidada,	140	68. Neptune,	84
19. Dreadnought,	98	44. Héros,	74	69. St. Justo,	74
20. Prince,	98	45. Duguy Trouin,	74	70. Hortense, f.	
21. Defence,	74	46. M. Blanc,	74	71. Flora, f.	
22. Thunderer,	74	47. Formidable,	80	72. Furet.	
23. Defiance,	74	48. St. Augustin,	74	73. Corneille, f.	
24. Spitfire,	74	49. Scipio,	74	74. Mercurio.	
25. Revenge,	74	50. Neptune,	84		

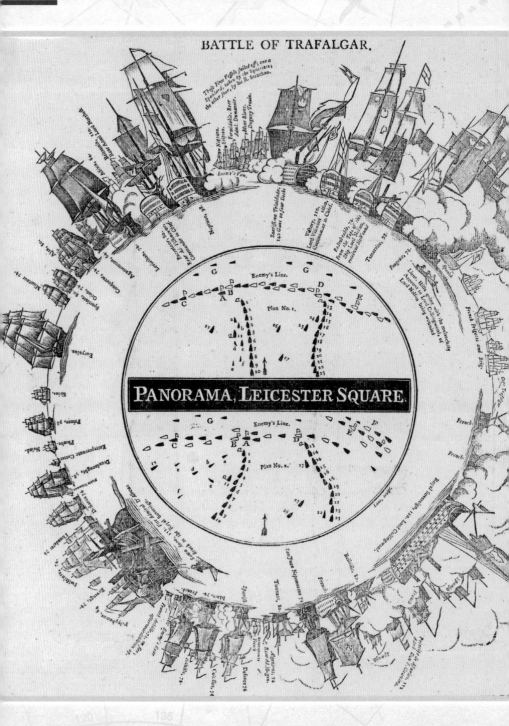

PANORAMA, LEICESTER SQUARE

Can you use the image to answer these questions?

1. What do the numbers found next to the names of each ship around the outside of the image specify? One of the ship's captions explains, if you need help.

2. Can you find the cape on the map that gave its name to the battle? What nationality are the ships pictured closest to it?

3. Where on the panorama can you find a rowing boat bearing bad news?

4. Which ship sounds like it should carry the King or Queen of the realm?

5. What is the name of the ship directly to the right of the ship that Rear Admiral Villeneuve commanded, as you look at the panorama?

6. Where on the panorama can you find a ship that shares its name with a Greek commander in Homer's *Iliad*, located next to a ship named after a biblical sea monster?

Opposite:
Henry Aston Barker created several panoramas, which were displayed at a specially designed venue in Leicester Square, London, with a central viewing platform. This viewing guide was designed to explain a panorama of the Battle of Trafalgar that was 30 feet high and 90 feet across.

MARITIME WEAPONRY

Iron cannonball, marked with the following: 'This shot entered the bow of the Victory at the glorious Battle of Trafalgar on the 21st October 1805 and lodged in the piece of timber in which it now lies.'

Can you solve these anagrams to reveal the names of seven weapons and types of ammunition used at sea? A description of each answer and the length of every word in it are given to help you. Note that any spacing in the anagrams may not match that of the solutions.

1. SPOILT (6)
  • A firearm used for close-range fighting, often carried alongside number 5 from this list.

2. FLIER (5)

- A type of gun designed to be accurate over a long distance. Lord Nelson received one as a gift from the Sultan of Turkey after the Battle of the Nile.

3. BASH ROT (3, 4)

- An elongated type of cannon-fired ammunition, a single one of which killed eight men on board the *Victory* during the Battle of Trafalgar.

4. NOT SHROUD (5, 4)

- A cannonball is an example of this type of ammunition.

5. TALCS US (7)

- A curved sword used for close-range fighting, often carried by sailors alongside number 1 from this list.

6. THEORIST (4, 4)

- A type of ammunition containing a collection of smaller shots, which disperse when fired.

7. HERO RIOT CHARTS (3, 4, 7)

- A device for transporting ammunition heated up to a very high temperature, which was used to set enemy ships on fire from a distance.

Bonus Questions:

a. What specifically does it mean to say that a ship has fired a 'broadside'?

b. In the Navy rating system for warships, what was the name given to a ship that carried eighty or more cannons spread over three gundecks? By the end of the nineteenth century this had increased to one hundred cannons.

The Battle of Trafalgar, 21 October 1805, *by J.M.W. Turner, 1822–1824*

TURNER'S BATTLE OF TRAFALGAR

The evocative image on the previous page shows the carnage and fury of a naval battle, with HMS *Victory* flying the signal flags for 'd'-'u'-'t'-'y', referencing Nelson's famous motto that 'England expects that every man will do his duty'.

Six ships are pictured in addition to the *Victory*. They are *Achille*, *Bucentaure*, *Neptune*, *Redoutable*, *Santissima Trinidad* and *Temeraire*. Can you use the painting, the introductory text and the statements below to work out which ship is which, and what nationality each ship is?

- Turner's image includes the moment when the *Redoutable* is finally taken and her crew have just surrendered. Nelson had been shot from the *Redoutable*.

- Four of the ships are French.

- The *Santissima Trinidad* is pictured further to the right than the *Bucentaure*.

- The *Redoutable* is on the opposite side of the painting to the other French ships.

- The *Temeraire* was also famously painted by Turner in a picture enjoyed by his British audience, *The Fighting Temeraire*.

- A Spanish ship, and one of the French ships, are pictured directly behind the *Victory*.

- The *Achille* is burning fiercely in the left half of the image.

- The *Bucentaure* is not the Spanish ship.

- The ship just emerging into view on the left-hand side of the painting is the *Neptune*.

CELEBRATING NELSON

Nelson's naval victories gave him heroic status in England, and many commemorative objects were created to celebrate his success. Eight of these objects are pictured on the following pages.

The names of each of these objects are given following the images, but they have been disguised. Can you delete one letter from each pair to reveal the actual names, then match each name with the correct image? A fact is included alongside each disguised name to help you.

1.

2.

3.

4.

5.

6.

7.

8.

A. TR OI BL BN OR NE
- This object connects to the Order of the Bath.

B. TN RO WO TL HE RP AI CK RK   OC AR TS OE
- This object was made in 1806 and features a velvet lining.

C. EP NA TG EC HL   MB OE XR
- This object was designed to hold small facial decorations.

D. DI NO MB EI LN TO   SB ON EX
- Part of this object is decorated with an image of a British sailor mourning in front of a bust of Nelson.

E. SC UC LR AT AR EI NT   RT HI ER
- This object commemorates the Battle of the Nile, one of the British Royal Navy's most famous victories under Nelson.

F. PC RI PO NE
- Nelson's hat forms the bowl of this object.

G. DM AO OC ER SL AT OR PT
- This object is based on a monument in Birmingham, built by Sir Richard Westmacott.

H. JP AI EP EN   ST AT ML PA EO AR
- This late nineteenth-century object could be used in conjunction with another of the objects shown.

RACE TO THE POLES

Hidden in the grid below are the names of six notable Arctic and Antarctic explorers. Reveal their names by drawing a continuous path that visits each square exactly once and never crosses itself, spelling out the names as it goes. The path can travel horizontally and vertically between touching letters, but never diagonally.

To help you, clues about the identity of the explorers are given below, with the number of letters in each name given in brackets. The names in the grid are found in the same order as the clues.

Your path should start at the 'in' arrow and end in the square with a flag in it.

J	E	S	E	T	O	E	R	T
A	M	C	L	K	N	B	A	F
K	O	O	A	C	R	O	L	C
E	R	N	H	T	T	O	N	O
S	D	E	S	R	O	C	S	⚑
E	N	S	T	L	A	O	H	N
N	U	M	A	D	N	J	N	I
M	T	H	H	E	O	R	F	L
A	T	E	W	N	S	A	N	K

1. This explorer was perhaps best known for his exploration of the Pacific Islands. He was killed on the island of Hawaii after attempting to kidnap the king. (5, 4)

2. This British explorer led the first attempts to traverse the Antarctic continent from the Weddell Sea to the Ross Sea. The *Endurance* was lost on his expedition after being crushed by sea ice. (6, 10)

3. This explorer led the *Discovery* expedition and, later, the *Terra Nova* expedition, from which none of the crew returned. (6, 6, 5)

4. This Norwegian explorer was the first person to reach the South Pole, in 1911. He later reached the North Pole too, making him the first person to have achieved both feats. (5, 8)

5. This explorer accompanied Robert Peary on Arctic expeditions over a period of around twenty years. The pair claimed to have been the first to reach the North Pole, in 1909. (7, 6)

6. This explorer led the Arctic exploration expeditions undertaken simultaneously by the ships HMS *Erebus* and HMS *Terror*. Neither ship returned from the voyage, which had been intended to navigate the Northwest Passage from the Atlantic to the Pacific oceans, travelling north of Canada. (4, 8)

POLAR WILDLIFE

'Ponko' the penguin, a stuffed toy modelled on photographic studies of penguins by Herbert Ponting, the expedition photographer on Robert Falcon Scott's Terra Nova expedition to the Ross Sea and South Pole between 1910 and 1913.

The exploration of Arctic and Antarctic waters revealed a plethora of wildlife previously unknown to British explorers, both above and below the ice.

Various facts about polar expeditions and how they interacted with wildlife are given below, but each of the sentences has had various key words removed. All of the missing words have been anagrammed and then placed in a group on the opposite page. Can you unscramble each word and restore it to its correct sentence? The number of letters in each missing word is indicated by the number of underlines shown.

1. The _ _ _ _ _ cribbage board below has been carved from a _ _ _ _ _ _ tusk. The underside of the board is engraved with part of the coastline of _ _ _ _ _ _ _ , and the top features several Arctic animals, including three _ _ _ _ _ and a _ _ _ _ _ _ _ _ _.

2. This watercolour was painted by Dr Alister Hardy, the _ _ _ _ _ _ _ _ on board the RRS *Discovery* during its exploration of the Antarctic. The painting focuses on _ _ _ _ _, and Hardy later became notable for his studies of the role of _ _ _ _ _ _ _ _ in the marine ecosystem, particularly in the diet of _ _ _ _ _ _ .

3. Some of the Arctic wildlife was later exploited. _ _ _ from whales was used to illuminate the streets of London, and their bones were used to make _ _ _ _ _ _ _ _ _, as well as form the structure of women's _ _ _ _ _ _ _ .

4. _ _ _ _ _ _ _ posed a huge problem to the territories where ships landed, as they were often stowaways, depleting astonishing amounts of local wildlife when they escaped. _ _ _ _ _ _ _ _ _ _ _ _ in Antarctica was finally declared free of these animals in 2018 after many years of failed eradication attempts.

AAAKLS	**ALOPR ABER**	**HOSTU AEGGIOR**
ABELLMRSU	**ALRSUW**	**IKLLR**
AEHLSW	**CEORSST**	**ILO**
AELSS	**DENORST**	**IORVY**
ALKNNOPT	**GILOOOSTZ**	

TRANS-ANTARCTIC EXPEDITIONS 1

The first overland crossing of the Antarctic continent was finally made in 1958, forty-six years after the first attempt in which the ship *Endurance* had been lost. Can you complete your own trans-Antarctic expedition by finding your way through the maze below? Your path can start at either arrow, but you must pass through the centre to reach the other side.

A distant bow view of Endurance *(1912) frozen into the ice floe, Weddell Sea, Antarctica.*

TRANS-ANTARCTIC EXPEDITIONS 2

Antarctic explorers look at the Sun, taken from the South Polar Times, *volume 2 (April–August 1903).*

Can you match each explorer (on the left) to the name of the trans-Antarctic expedition (on the right) they led?

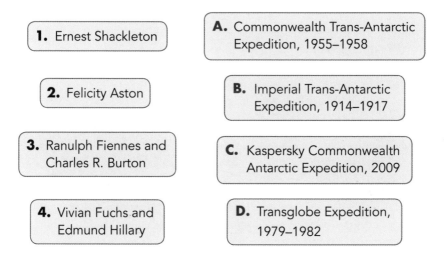

1. Ernest Shackleton

A. Commonwealth Trans-Antarctic Expedition, 1955–1958

2. Felicity Aston

B. Imperial Trans-Antarctic Expedition, 1914–1917

3. Ranulph Fiennes and Charles R. Burton

C. Kaspersky Commonwealth Antarctic Expedition, 2009

4. Vivian Fuchs and Edmund Hillary

D. Transglobe Expedition, 1979–1982

Bonus Question:

Which of these expeditions was completed entirely on skis?

FIVE JOURNEYS OF PRIMARY EXPLORERS

Between 1487–1502, five notable explorers set out from Europe by boat:

- Bartholomew Dias
- Amerigo Vespucci
- Vasco da Gama
- Christopher Columbus
- John Cabot

During this period, it had become clear that it was possible to sail around Africa into the Indian Ocean, and that America was a separate continent and not in fact part of Asia.

The journeys of these five notable explorers are all marked on this map, with the approximate path of each route drawn in a different colour.

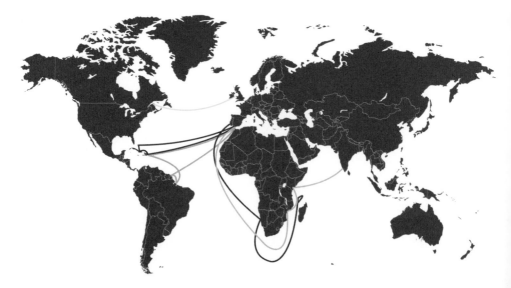

Use the map and the statements below to work out which explorer's journey each coloured line represents, and each explorer's nationality.

- Some of the explorers are Italian

- A Portuguese explorer visited Namibia, then travelled to the Indian Ocean before being forced to turn back

- All of the explorers who travelled to the Americas were the same nationality

- Christopher Columbus sailed to the Caribbean and visited the Bahamas, Haiti and the Dominican Republic

- Amerigo Vespucci did not travel to Newfoundland

- Vasco da Gama followed a similar route to Bartholomew Dias, but successfully reached India, becoming the first European to do so

- John Cabot was the same nationality as Christopher Columbus

- The explorer who followed the blue line was Portuguese

THE VOYAGE OF THE MAYFLOWER

Coin commemorating the Pilgrim Tercentenary celebration, 1920.

In 1620, a group of Puritans left England on board the *Mayflower*. They sailed to America to found a new colony, away from the religious persecution they felt they faced in Britain, and landed in the area of modern-day Massachusetts. Around half of the Pilgrim Fathers, as they were known, died during the first winter.

Can you complete more of the story by filling in the missing words below? Each word can be restored by joining two or more of the fragments shown opposite. Each fragment is used once, the number of letters in each missing word is given.

1. The Pilgrims were aiming to land in the Colony of Virginia, where they had permission to make their home, but were forced to anchor at _____ _____ due to bad winter weather. (4,3)

2. They named their settlement _____ Colony, after the port they had set out from in England. (8)

3. The youngest passenger on the *Mayflower* was just one year old and travelled from Leiden, Holland. Her name was _____ Cooper, and she shared her first name with a personality trait. (8)

4. A boy was born during the *Mayflower's* journey across the Atlantic Ocean, to Elizabeth Hopkins and her husband Stephen. He was named _____, reflecting his place of birth. (7)

5. The first European child born in the Pilgrims' settlement was named _____, meaning 'pilgrim', or 'coming from another country'. He also shared his name with a bird. (9)

6. A Native American known as _____ helped the Pilgrims liaise with the indigenous populations. (7)

7. The settlers created a document known as the Mayflower _____, setting out how the colony should be governed. (7)

AN	**CA**	**COD**	**COM**
EGR	**HUM**	**ILI**	**INE**
MOU	**NUS**	**OCEA**	**PACT**
PE	**PER**	**PLY**	**SQU**
TH	**TO**	**TY**	

SIR MARTIN FROBISHER

Engraving of Sir Martin Frobisher by M. van der Gucht.

Sir Martin Frobisher (1535–1594) set out in 1576 to look for the Northwest Passage, a navigable northern passage between the Atlantic and Pacific oceans. Instead, he arrived in what is now Canada and discovered what he thought was gold ore contained in rocks. He took home 200 tons of it, and then returned for another 1,350 tons. Unfortunately, it turned out to be relatively worthless.

Can you answer these multiple-choice questions about Frobisher's voyages? To help you work it out, each letter is used once in total.

1. What were the rocks Frobisher brought back from Canada eventually found to contain?
   a. Iron pyrite
   b. Silver ore
   c. Graphite
   d. Chalk

2. Frobisher compared the size of the lump of rock he brought back from his first trip to Canada to what object?
   a. A wine barrel
   b. A poodle
   c. A dinner plate
   d. A loaf of bread

3. What is the modern-day name of the north-eastern Canadian island where Frobisher landed on his first voyage to search for the Northwest Passage?
   a. Vancouver Island
   b. Graham Island
   c. Baffin Island
   d. Frob's Island

4. What did Elizabeth I name the island that Frobisher encountered? The name translates into English as 'unknown boundary'.
   a. Terra Nova
   b. Meta Incognita
   c. Sinus Tonitralis
   d. Annus Horribilis

SIR FRANCIS DRAKE

Sir Francis Drake was an
Elizabethan explorer who
was famous for many
deeds, but in particular for
his circumnavigation of the
world in a single expedition,
from 1577 to 1580. He was
also second-in-command
of the English fleet against
the Spanish Armada.

*Sir Francis Drake, by Marcus
Gheeraerts the Younger, c.1591.*

SHIP NAMES
Unscramble the letters in the anagrams below to reveal the names
of the five ships that left Plymouth on 13 December 1577 for
Drake's circumnavigation of the world. Each ship name is a type of
bird, a first name, or a type of flower, and all the names consist of a
single word.

1. SAWN
2. A PENCIL
3. HAZEL BITE
4. GRIM LOAD
5. SHORTER CHIP

Bonus Question:
Which of these ships did Drake personally sail in during
the voyage?

QUIZ

1. To what did Drake famously rename his ship during his round-
the-world voyage?
a. The *Swiftbird*
b. The *Lancaster*
c. The *Golden Hinde*

2. Where in today's London can a recreation of this vessel be
found?
a. Near Greenwich Park
b. Near London Bridge
c. Near Tower Bridge

3. Which game was Francis Drake said to be playing when the
Spanish Armada was sighted off the south coast of England?
a. Bowls
b. Tennis
c. Cards

4. In which modern US state is the area that Drake named 'Nova
Albion' during his circumnavigation of the world?
a. Florida
b. California
c. North Carolina

SIR WALTER RALEIGH

Walter Raleigh was an ambitious sailor, poet and explorer, who gained popularity in the court of Elizabeth I through his voyages and writing. He fell in and out of favour in court, and his secret marriage to Elizabeth Throckmorton, one of Elizabeth I's ladies-in-waiting, was conducted without the Queen's permission, leading to his imprisonment in the Tower of London in 1592.

Engraving of Sir Walter Raleigh by George Vertue.

Can you rearrange the letters opposite to reveal the answers to the following five questions about Raleigh's life? Each letter is used only once, and each answer is a single word.

1. Which addictive substance did Raleigh popularise in the English court?

2. What type of vegetable is Raleigh said to have introduced to Britain?

3. Raleigh led an expedition to find the legendary city of El Dorado in 1594. What was the city said to be filled with?

4. What name was given to the area of America to which Raleigh financed a voyage in the late 1500s?

5. What did Raleigh's wife Elizabeth shorten her name to?

SIR JAMES LANCASTER

Sir James Lancaster, painted in 1596.

James Lancaster was the first commander of the East India Company, playing a key part in the establishment of trade alliances in Asia, which led to importing many new spices and other goods back to England.

In the following list of islands, countries and bays to which James Lancaster travelled on his voyages, every other letter is missing. Can you restore the missing letters to reveal the places he visited?

1. J__V__

2. __R__Z__L

3. S__M__T__A

4. __A__Z__B__R

5. T__B__E   __A__

6. N__C__B__R   __S__A__D__

Bonus Question:

What did James Lancaster give as a treatment for scurvy to the men on his ship?

a. Exercise

b. Lemon juice

c. Wine

d. Beer

EDWARD BARLOW'S JOURNAL

Pages of Edward Barlow's journal documenting his adventurous life at sea. The journal was acquired by the National Maritime Museum in 1939.

Edward Barlow was eighteen when he became a naval apprentice on the *Naseby*, an eighty-gun ship of the line in the British Navy, which was later renamed the *Royal Charles*. His more than forty-year-long career as a sailor took him to many locations, which he wrote about in a journal from 1659–1703.

Six of the places Barlow visited – all beginning with the letter 'B' – have been concealed in the coded puzzle below, although each letter of their names has been replaced with a number.

Can you work out which number has been assigned to which letter and crack the code to reveal the names? Extra clues about the locations have been given, and a blank guide has been provided to help you keep track of the letters you decode. Some of the letters are already filled to get you started.

Letters to use: **A B D E G I L M N O R S T V Y Z**

1	2	3	4	5	6	7	8	9	10	11	12	13	14	15	16
B	Z											V			

An island country in the Caribbean

1	6	11	1	6	2	12	10
B			B				

This was the historical name for Jakarta, in Indonesia

1	6	16	6	13	9	6
B				V		

This South Asian region is divided between India and Bangladesh

1	15	5	8	6	7
B					

This is now Norway's second-largest city

1	15	11	8	15	5
B					

This Indian city is now known as Mumbai

1	12	14	1	6	4
B			B		

A South American country

1	11	6	3	9	7
B			Z		

Bonus Question:

Edward Barlow wrote in his journal that a rhino was brought back to England from one of his voyages, and then sold. How much did it sell for, according to Barlow?

a. Around £500
b. Around £1,500
c. Around £2,000

LOCATIONS NAMED AFTER SEAFARERS

Engraving of Ferdinand Magellan by Nicolas de Larmessin.

The names of some notable seafarers can be found across the globe, preserved in the modern names of places they encountered. The locations of eight particular namesakes are shown on the map opposite, marked with a letter. Using the map and your general knowledge, can you work out which country, island, city or passage each letter indicates, and which explorer from the list below they take their name from? Each lettered location matches with exactly one explorer.

FERDINAND MAGELLAN   CHRISTOPHER COLUMBUS

JAMES COOK   JOHN MARSHALL

FRANCIS DRAKE   GEORGE VANCOUVER

TRISTÃO DA CUNHA   JUAN DE BERMÚDEZ

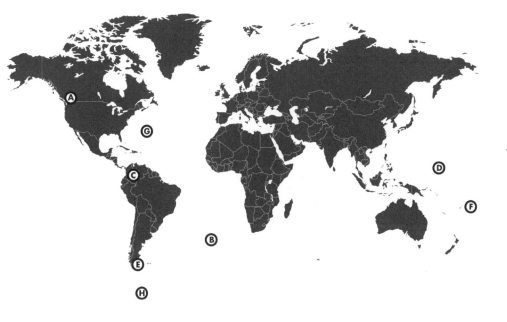

Bonus Question:

Which of these explorers was responsible for naming
the Pacific Ocean?

TRADE ROUTES

In the eighteenth century a series of trade routes criss-crossed the Atlantic, using prevailing winds and currents, allowing goods and raw materials to circulate.

A painting showing Bristol docks on the River Avon. The ship in the foreground on the left is unloading timber from America. Painted by Joseph Walter, 1834.

All vowels have been removed from each product in these lists of imports and exports that were transported along different Atlantic trade routes between 1768–72. Can you restore the vowels to the products, then match each list or individual product to the correct trade route? Each product is one word only, and extra spaces have been introduced to try to throw you off track.

IMPORTS/EXPORTS	TRADE ROUTES
F SH	Britain to North America and West Indies
SGR ML SSS RM	Canada to Europe
WN	Europe to North America
LVS TCK WD	North America to Britain
SG R C FF CT TN	North America to West Indies
TX TLS MT LW RK	West Indies to Britain
TB CC NDG RC	West Indies to North America

Bonus Question:

Approximately how many miles shorter did the journey from England to China become after the Suez Canal was opened in 1869?

a. 2,500 miles
b. 3,000 miles
c. 4,500 miles

THE EAST INDIA COMPANY: SPICE

The East India Company was established at the end of the seventeenth century and was given a charter by Elizabeth I, which referred to it as 'The Governor and Company of Merchants of London Trading into the East-Indies'.

The East India Company's original aim was to bring spices back from India to sell in London, but they soon expanded into tea and textiles, exerting influence on British fashions during the 1700s. 'East Indiamen', as the company ships were known, were some of the largest ships of their era.

Original entrance to the East India Docks. The tea, silks and spices that arrived from the east would be sent by horse and cart along Commercial Road to the East India Company's Cutler Street warehouses in the City of London.

THE SPICE ISLANDS

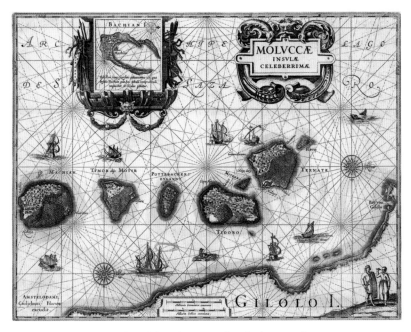

Map of Maluku, decorated with ships and sea creatures, created by Willem Blaeu, c.1640.

The Maluku region of modern-day Indonesia was famed for its spice production, which is why the archipelago was named 'the Spice Islands' when first visited by English ships in the early 1600s.

The names of six of the islands in the Maluku region are given overleaf, but they have each been mixed with the name of a modern Asian country that has the same number of letters. Can you work out which letter in each pair belongs to the modern Asian country, and which letter in each pair belongs to an island in Maluku, and thus reveal all of the pairs of names?

1. LB UA OR SU

2. IS NE DR IA AM

3. AC MH IB NO NA

4. BT IH UD TO RA EN

5. TV IE ER NT AN AT EM

6. IH NA LD OM NA EH ES RI AA

Bonus Question:
In 1622, the East India Company ship *Charles* arrived in London
with 800,000 pounds of pepper, which at the time was worth
£73,000. How much do you think that would be worth in today's
money?

a. £5,800,000
b. £10,700,000
c. £12,400,000

HIDDEN SPICES
Can you find the names of five spices imported by the East India
Company concealed in the following culinary-themed sentences?
    As an example, *salt* is hidden in the phrase:

'This dish need**s alt**ernative seasoning'.

1. I can't bear a hazelnut, me. Go and get me some almonds.

2. I only gave the dessert card a momentary glance – did you see anything you liked?

3. Eric loves the new restaurant that opened around the corner.

4. I hear from a certain someone that there will be a professional chef joining us for dinner.

5. Will you be eating at the Almanac Inn? A Monday is definitely the best night to go.

Once you have revealed the names of the spices, can you answer the following questions on their history and uses? No spice is used more than once.

a. Which of these spices was known as the 'Queen of Spices'?
b. Which of these spices was a common toothache remedy?
c. Which of these spices was used medicinally to fight indigestion, colds and diabetes?

THE EAST INDIA COMPANY: TEA

A sketch showing workers unloading tea ships in the East India Docks, 1867. Tea was first brought from China to Britain in the 1670s as a medicinal herb, and was slow to become a popular drink. It was only when it was sweetened with sugar that it began to appeal to British taste.

The East India Company imported tea from China and, as more people were introduced to it in the 1700s, it became immensely popular. Indeed, by the late 1700s, most of the company's profits came from tea.

Seven types of tea that were imported by the East India Company have all been encoded opposite using the same system, where the numbers represent letters in the alphabet. Can you figure out what the system is and therefore decode the types of tea?

1. 16511155

2. 191521381514

3. 3151471521

4. 215851

5. 29147

6. 825191514

7. 1991471215

Once you have decoded the names, can you answer the following questions?

1. Of the names given above, how many of the teas are varieties of black tea, and how many are varieties of green tea?

2. Which of these teas was the most expensive of its kind, and was also known as 'imperial tea'?

3. In 1701, the East India Company imported enough tea to brew around 4 million pots. How many pots do you think they could have brewed from their imports in 1801?

   a. 350 million pots
   b. 650 million pots
   c. 950 million pots

THE EAST INDIA COMPANY: TEXTILES

Many different kinds of fabric were produced in India and then imported to Great Britain by the East India Company. Can you restore the names of eight different types of fibre and fabric below, which have each had any letters found in the word 'INDIGO' removed? The number of letters in each solution is given to help you. For example, 'GREEN' would have had the G and N removed to form 'REE'.

1.   SLK (4)

2.   CTT (6)

3.   LE (5)

4.   CHTZ (6)

5.   MUSL (6)

6.   CALC (6)

7.   KAT (4)

8.   HAM (7)

Once you have restored the names, can you match each of the eight fibres and fabrics to a correct description below? Each fibre or fabric matches with exactly one description.

A. This lightweight fabric can be used as a filter in cooking

B. This fabric usually has a checked pattern

C. This fabric is usually unbleached and plain white in colour

D. This fibre is produced by the caterpillar of a particular kind of moth

E. This fibre can be harvested from around the seeds of a tropical plant

F. This fabric is made from the stalks of the plant that produces linseed

G. This fabric gains its appearance from the yarn being tie-dyed before it is woven

H. This printed and glazed fabric first originated in India

Bonus Question:

The East India Company brought back £46,494 worth of textiles from Asia in 1704, which it sold in Britain for £311,299, making a profit of £264,805. What is this profit worth in today's money?

a. £12 million
b. £27 million
c. £39 million

SOLUTIONS

History Makers and Record Breakers

c. 1000   Leifur Eiríksson lands at Vinland – the first known voyage from Europe to mainland North America

1773   James Cook's ship the *Resolution* is the first known ship to cross the Antarctic Circle

1875   Matthew Webb completes the first known unaided swim across the English Channel

1896   Frank Samuelson and George Harbo are the first to row across the Atlantic, doing so in 55 days

1898   Joshua Slocum completes the first solo circumnavigation of the world

1993   Ann Bancroft becomes the first woman to have visited both the North and South Poles

2019   Victor Vescovo is the first person to dive to Challenger Deep – the deepest part of the World Ocean.

Maritime Women

1. IDA LEWIS
2. GRACE DARLING
3. HANNAH SNELL
4. MARY LACY
5. MARY PATTEN

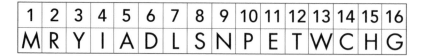

1	2	3	4	5	6	7	8	9	10	11	12	13	14	15	16
M	R	Y	I	A	D	L	S	N	P	E	T	W	C	H	G

Nelson Crossword

Nelson Quiz
1. b. 12 years old
2. c. St Paul's Cathedral
3. a. 20
4. b. 4
5. c. A polar bear
6. a. The mast of *L'Orient*, a French ship devastated at the Battle of the Nile

The Battle of Trafalgar – Battle Plan
1. 73 – 17 – 16 – 49 – 46 draws a 'P' on the map
2. 65 – 37 – 67 – 60 – 56 draws an 'A' on the map
3. 19 – 23 – 36 – 31 – 61 – 56 draws an 'S' on the map

4. 39 – 30 – 66 – 67 draws a 'C' on the map

5. 43 – 12 – 48 – 72 – 43 draws an 'O' on the map

The letters spell out PASCO. John Pasco was the signal officer on board HMS *Victory* during the Battle of Trafalgar.

Panorama, Leicester Square

1. The number next to each name indicates the number of guns carried by each ship.

2. French – 'Cape Trafalgar' is the area of land that gave the Battle of Trafalgar its name, and can be found on the right-hand side of the panorama. The labels 'French Frigates and Brig.' and 'French' can be found on either side of it.

3. Towards the top-right of the panorama, next to the label 'Fougeux, 74.'. There is a label beneath an image of a rowing boat saying, 'Lieut. Hills going with the melancholy Account to Lord Collingwood, of Lord Nelson being wounded'.

4. *Royal Sovereign*, found at the bottom-right of the panorama.

5. *Neptune*. This ship is directly next to the ship labelled '*Bucentaur*, 80. Rear Ad. Villeneuve, Commander in Chief.' It can be found near the top of the panorama.

6. At the top-left of the panorama. The ship named after a Greek commander in Homer's *Iliad* is *Agamemnon*, while the ship named after a biblical sea monster is *Leviathan*.

Maritime Weaponry

1. PISTOL

2. RIFLE

3. BAR SHOT

4. ROUND SHOT

5. CUTLASS

6. TIER SHOT

7. HOT SHOT CARRIER

Bonus Questions:

a. To fire a broadside means to fire all the guns on one side of a ship simultaneously.

b. A First Rate ship.

Turner's Battle of Trafalgar

From left to right the ships (other than HMS *Victory*) are:

- *Neptune*   French
- *Achille*   French
- *Bucentaure*   French
- *Santissima Trinidad*   Spanish
- *Redoutable*   French
- *Temeraire*   British

Celebrating Nelson

A. RIBBON – 2 (featuring the motto of the Order of the Bath)

B. TOOTHPICK CASE – 7

C. PATCH BOX – 8 (used for applying false beauty marks)

D. DOMINO BOX – 1

E. CURTAIN TIE – 5

F. PIPE – 3

G. DOORSTOP – 6

H. PIPE TAMPER – 4

Race to the Poles

1. JAMES COOK

2. ERNEST SHACKLETON

3. ROBERT FALCON SCOTT

4. ROALD AMUNDSEN

5. MATTHEW HENSON

6. JOHN FRANKLIN

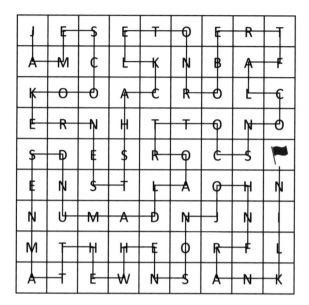

Polar Wildlife

The unscrambled words, in order of their appearance in each sentence, are as follows:

1. IVORY
  WALRUS
  ALASKA
  SEALS
  POLAR BEAR
2. ZOOLOGIST
  KRILL
  PLANKTON
  WHALES
3. OIL
  UMBRELLAS
  CORSETS
4. RODENTS
  SOUTH GEORGIA

Trans-Antarctic Expeditions 1

Trans-Antarctic Expeditions 2

1. B
2. C
3. D
4. A

Bonus Question: The Kaspersky Commonwealth Antarctic Expedition was completed on skis. It was also an all-female expedition.

Five Journeys of Primary Explorers

EXPLORER:	NATIONALITY:	ROUTE COLOUR:
Bartholomew Dias	Portuguese	▬▬▬ Purple
Amerigo Vespucci	Italian	▬▬ Green
Vasco da Gama	Portuguese	▬▬ Blue
Christopher Columbus	Italian	▬▬ Pink
John Cabot	Italian	▬▬ Yellow

The Voyage of the Mayflower

1. CAPE COD
2. PLYMOUTH
3. HUMILITY
4. OCEANUS
5. PEREGRINE
6. SQUANTO
7. COMPACT

Sir Martin Frobisher

1. a – Iron pyrite (also known as 'fool's gold')
2. d – A loaf of bread
3. c – Baffin Island. Vancouver Island and Graham Island are both on the west coast of Canada.
4. b – Meta Incognita

Sir Francis Drake

Ship names
1. Swan
2. Pelican
3. Elizabeth
4. Marigold
5. Christopher
Bonus Question: The Pelican

Quiz

1. c – The *Golden Hinde*
2. b – Near London Bridge
3. a – Bowls
4. b – California

Sir Walter Raleigh

1. TOBACCO
2. POTATO
3. GOLD
4. VIRGINIA
5. BESS

Sir James Lancaster

1. JAVA
2. BRAZIL
3. SUMATRA
4. ZANZIBAR
5. TABLE BAY
6. NICOBAR ISLANDS

Bonus Question: b. Lemon juice, and it was effective too – the Admiralty finally accepted his report that it helped . . . 200 years later.

Edward Barlow's Journal

1. BARBADOS
2. BATAVIA
3. BENGAL
4. BERGEN
5. BOMBAY
6. BRAZIL

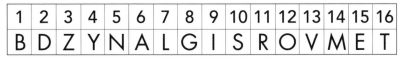

1	2	3	4	5	6	7	8	9	10	11	12	13	14	15	16
B	D	Z	Y	N	A	L	G	I	S	R	O	V	M	E	T

Bonus Question: c. Around £2,000 – or just over £400,000 in today's money.

Locations Named After Seafarers

A. Vancouver – Canadian city named after English naval officer George Vancouver

B. Tristan da Cunha – British Overseas Territory named after Portuguese explorer Tristão da Cunha

C. Colombia – South American country named after Italian explorer Christopher Columbus

D. Marshall Islands – Micronesian island country named after English explorer John Marshall

E. Strait of Magellan – South American navigational passage named after Portuguese explorer Ferdinand Magellan

F. Cook Islands – South Pacific island country named after English explorer James Cook

G. Bermuda – British Overseas Territory named after Spanish navigator Juan de Bermúdez

H. Drake Passage – Body of water between South America and Antarctica named after English privateer Francis Drake

Bonus Question: Ferdinand Magellan named the Pacific Ocean. Specifically, he called it the *Mar Pacífico*, meaning 'peaceful sea'.

Trade Routes

IMPORTS/EXPORTS	TRADE ROUTES
FISH	Canada to Europe
SUGAR, MOLASSES, RUM	West Indies to North America
WINE	Europe to North America
LIVESTOCK, WOOD	North America to West Indies
SUGAR, COFFEE, COTTON	West Indies to Britain
TEXTILES, METALWORK	Britain to North America and West Indies
TOBACCO, INDIGO, RICE	North America to Britain

Bonus Question: B – the route became 3,000 miles shorter

The East India Company: Spice

The Spice Islands

1. Island: BURU
   Country: LAOS
2. Island: SERAM
   Country: INDIA
3. Island: AMBON
   Country: CHINA
4. Island: TIDORE
   Country: BHUTAN
5. Island: TERNATE
   Country: VIETNAM
6. Island: HALMAHERA
   Country: INDONESIA

Bonus Question: b. The value of the pepper brought over on the Charles would be around £10,700,000 today.

Hidden Spices

1. Nutmeg – I can't bear a hazel**nut**, **me**. **G**o and get me some almonds.
2. Cardamom – I only gave the dessert **card a mom**entary glance – did you see anything you liked?
3. Cloves – Eri**c** **loves** the new restaurant that opened around the corner.
4. Mace – I hear fro**m a ce**rtain someone that there will be a professional chef joining us for dinner.
5. Cinnamon – Will you be eating at the Almana**c** **Inn**? **A Mon**day is definitely the best night to go.

a. Cardamom
b. Cloves
c. Cinnamon

The East India Company: Tea

A has been replaced with 1, B with 2 and so on up until Z with 26. Then all of the spaces between numbers have been removed, so it is part of solving the puzzle to work out which digits go together to make which numbers. The correct numbers are shown separated with hyphens below:

1. 16-5-11-15-5: PEKOE
2. 19-15-21-3-8-15-14: SOUCHON
3. 3-15-14-7-15-21: CONGOU
4. 2-15-8-5-1: BOHEA
5. 2-9-14-7: BING
6. 8-25-19-15-14: HYSON
7. 19-9-14-7-12-15: SINGLO

Additional Questions:

1. The first four names are black tea varieties, and the final three are green tea varieties
2. Bing tea – a green tea variety and number 5 in the list - was also known as imperial tea
3. c. In 1801, the East India Company imported enough tea to brew around 950 million pots

The East India Company: Textiles

1. SILK
2. COTTON
3. LINEN
4. CHINTZ
5. MUSLIN
6. CALICO
7. IKAT
8. GINGHAM

A. Muslin
B. Gingham
C. Calico
D. Silk
E. Cotton
F. Linen
G. Ikat
H. Chintz

Bonus Question: c. £39 million

CHAPTER 5

MAPS

The National Maritime Museum holds a vast collection of manuscripts and printed hydrography (charts), cartography (maps) and written sailing directions (originally known as 'portolans'). The collection dates from the sixteenth to the twentieth century, and comprises tens of thousands of items, with only a small selection featuring in the following chapter.* Stretch your razor-sharp observational skills and rely on your general knowledge to analyse and decipher the selection of maps on the following pages – it's the ultimate navigational challenge!

* A note on maps: maps are an interpretation of what they depict and should be regarded as historical documents. As such, they can present a biased view of the world.

COMPASS VARIATION – Edmond Halley

The chart on the following pages shows the results of the first purely scientific British state-sponsored expedition to record variations in the earth's magnetic field. The field is not uniform and so a mariner's compass points either side of north to a variable degree depending on the ship's position. To make navigation safer, Halley made an extensive series of comparisons between compass readings and determinations of north by astronomical observation. He plotted what are referred to as 'isogonic lines', joining points of equal magnetic variation.

1. The ornate shield superimposed on north Africa dedicates the map to a prominent early eighteenth-century public figure.
   a. What relation was he to the English sovereign at the time the map was published?
   b. Of which military organisation was he the ceremonial leader?

2. a. Which scientific field (other than that for which this map is related) was Edmond Halley well known for in his day?
   b. Which celestial object is named after him?

3. a. Which island country did Portuguese navigators name after a Roman martyr who is patron saint of cooks and archivists? Both its historical and modern name are given on the map.
   b. How many isogonic lines of variation are drawn through the island identified above, and what degrees of variation from north do they show?

4. What is the degree of variation from true north indicated by the isogonic line that passes through both of the following:

- A country depicted in the approximate area of the modern-day Russian Kamchatka peninsula, and described on this map as having been discovered in 1643.
- A land mass joining two large countries with Latin names, depicted on this map as sharing one coastline but now known to be separated by the Torres Strait.

5. Which large country on the map is labelled with both its modern-day name and that of a medieval principality, which gave its name to the country's current capital city?

6. What name is given to the Adriatic Sea on this map? It has a strong Italian connection.

7. The interestingly named 'Tooth Coast' is shown marked on the west African seaboard on this map.
  a. To which modern-day country do you think this best corresponds?
  b. Approximately how many degrees of variation from north would you read from your compass at the area named 'Gold Coast', which can be found just east of 'Tooth Coast'?
  c. The meaning of 'Gold Coast' is self-apparent, but what do you think gave the 'Tooth Coast' its name?

8. Can you find a place on the African coast that shares its name (ignoring spaces) with a modern-day country in the Balkan region? It translates into English as 'black mountain'.

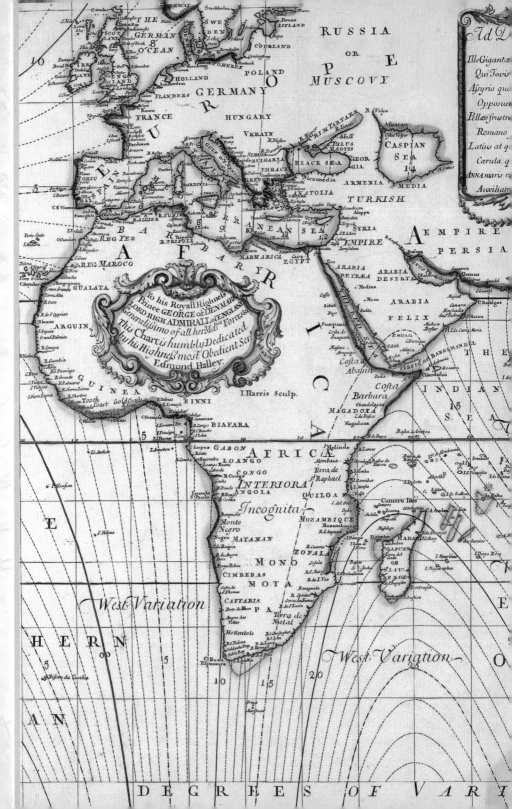

A magnetic chart produced by Edmond Halley in 1702.

WORLD MAP – Pierre Du Val

The map on the following pages shows part of a world map created by Pierre Du Val in 1686. The map includes several major trade routes that were in operation at the time. Can you use the map and your general knowledge to answer the following questions?

1. a. A 'prime meridian' is labelled in French on this map. What colour has been used to highlight it, and which two lines of latitude drawn on the map intersect with its French label?

b. What is the modern-day name of the country that is intersected by both the prime meridian and the line demarking the Arctic Circle on the map?

c. Which line of longitude on this map roughly corresponds to the present-day prime meridian, also known as the Greenwich meridian?

2. a. An archipelago of islands is shown some distance west of Portugal, labelled with their name in Portuguese. What is the modern English name of these islands?

b. What rich fishing ground can be found north-west of this archipelago, between the 330th and 340th lines of longitude? The label is in French.

3. Between which two lines of longitude on this map can you find an island that lends its name to a notorious triangle? Its modern-day capital is Hamilton.

4. The full map includes
the following key:

Translations of the routes shown are as follows, reading from top
to bottom:

- Route to the West Indies
- Route back from the West Indies
- Route to the East Indies
- Route back from the East Indies

Use the key and the map to answer the following questions:

a. A ship is shown bound for the West Indies. What line of
latitude on the map does its illustration overlap?

b. Which saint features in the name of the island immediately
west of the ship shown returning from the East Indies?

c. Which island, now a British Overseas Territory, will soon be
passed by the ship shown on its way to the East Indies?

Next page:
World map by French geographer Pierre Du Val in 1686.

TERRES
Baye
de Baffins

Lancaster
Sound

A

I. de Cumberland

Vieux-G

M.Rale

C.Horn

Sander soun

Destroit de Dau

Cercle du Pole Arctique

Nouveau Danemarq

New Nort

New Soute walles

Mer Christiane

Port de Munk

Buttons Bay

Destroit de Hudson

Forest d'York

I. de Forbisu

C.Fare

Port Nel son

Golfe de Hudson

CANADA ou NOUVELLE FRANCE

C.Bro

Terre de la Croix Iesso

Destroit d'Anien

Blanc C.Mendo cino

AMERIQUE SEPTEMTRIONALE

Lac Superieur
Lac de Puans

Saguenay
Quebec
3 Rivieres
Montreal
Boston
Manhate

I.de Rey

I.Neu

Mont Royal

C.de Su

NOUVEAU MEXIQUE

S.Fe

FLORIDE

VIRGINIE
Pomeiok

C.S.Luc

C.California

MEXIQUE

Danuco

S.Mathi

I.Bermudes

MER DE NO

Golfe de

Tropique de Car

I.Lucaye
C.Manahani

les Moines

la Voxina
la digraciee

Villoa

S.Thomas

Mexico
Mechoacan

Mexi

Vera-Cruz

P.Rico
I.Tortue

Lama que

ISLES ANTIL LES

S.Christophe
Gadaloupe

P.Rico

la Nublada

Rocca Partida

Guatimala

Truxillo

N.ESPAN

Barba

les Moines

MER PACIFIQUE autrement

L.S.Pierre

Barbudos

los Vadadores

Panama

Coman

Manoa

TERRE-FERME
Orenoqu

C.de Nord

GUAYANA

chipel S. gare lardines

Cord les Res Paxaros

200 210 220 230 240 250 260 270 280 290

Equateur ou

L.Puna

l'Amazone ou Orellane

l'Orenoqu

Cogemim

Schouten

Nom de Iesus

Isabelle

I.de Salomon

I.Horn
I.Iacquer
I.de bonne Esperance

I.Cocos
I.des traitres
I.des Mouches

l.deau

I.Sans fond

I.des Chiens

Truxillo
PE ROU

Cusco
Lima

Arica

Potosi

Tobiso

AMERIQUE MERIDIONA

Br

guinee

C.de la Cr

I.Roterdam

I.Midelburg I.Amsterdam

L.S.Pedro

Paraguai

l'Assumpt

Tropique de Capricorne

L.S.Ambroise
L.S.Felipe

L.S.Iago del Estero
la Serena
S.Iago
Valparaiso
I.Iean Fernand
la Mocha

CHILI
la Concepcion
la Imperial
Baldivia
Osorno

La PLA
PLAT

TUCUMAN

Buenos

MER DE SUD

I.du Roy

N.le Zelande

C.Boreel

Terre de Qvir

MAGEL LANIQUE
Port desire

B.S. Iulien

MAG

S.Felippe

Magellan

Terre de Feu

le Maire

Destroit de

Destroit des Estats de Brower

Passage

WORLD MAP – Pierre Hamon

The map on the following pages is a mid-16th-century world map by Pierre Hamon, which includes a speculative geography of the South Pacific. Please note that on this map, 'J' is written as 'I', and 'U' as 'V'.

1. What is most unusual about the way this world map has been drawn?

2. a. Can you find two labels on this map that both translate into English as 'southern sea'? It might help to know that one modern country name comes from the Latin for 'southern'.

  b. What are the modern names of the two oceans indicated by the labels in part 'a'?

3. a. Given the map, and your answer to question '2a', which cardinal point do you think 'septentrionale' refers to, in the label 'MER SEPTENTRIONALE'?

  b. And what is its modern name?

4. Which modern Indonesian island did Marco Polo describe as the largest island in the world, as implied by the name shown on this map?

5. Can you identify which labels on the map indicate each of the following?

  a. An unknown or unexplored area

  b. An area of Africa whose name stems from the Greek for 'foreigner', and which became associated with pirates in

Europe due to raids led by corsairs from the area in the sixteenth century

c. An area of the Atlantic Ocean with a name that reveals the mapmaker's nationality and inherent bias?

6. Can you find an island that sounds like it might have been encountered by Gulliver on his travels? Although the label is in French, the key word is similar to its English equivalent.

7. Pontus was an ancient region of Asia located on the southern edge of a body of water labelled on this map as 'Mer pontique', shown in the close-up opposite. What is the modern-day English name for this body of water?

8. The 'Monts de la Lune' (Mountains of the Moon), pictured in the close-up opposite, are a legendary mountain range mentioned by Ptolemy as being the source of which river?

9. What do you notice about the representation of Greenland, pictured in the close-up below, compared to what is known of its modern geography?

World map by Pierre Hamon.

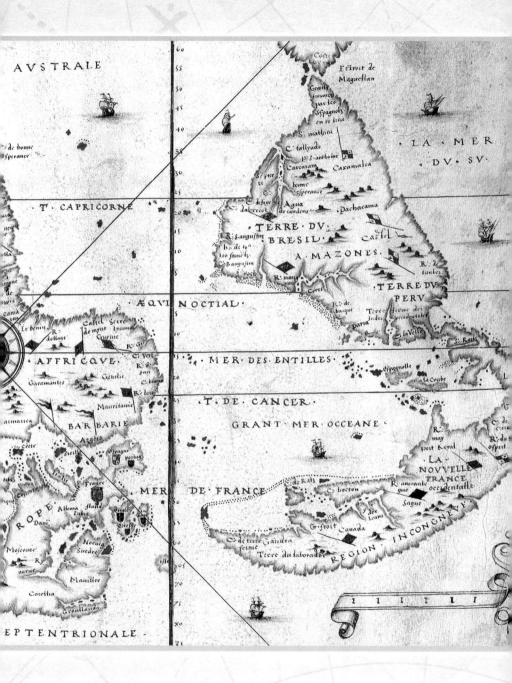

EAST INDIES – Pieter Goos

The map on the following pages is by Dutch cartographer Pieter Goos, made in the 1600s at the height of the Dutch trading empire. Contemporary Dutch navigators wished to bypass traditional overland trade routes, and maps like this one provided details of alternative maritime routes. The routes on this map were based on the latest explorations of south-east Asia and Oceania.

1. Four of the illustrated ships on the map can be seen to be flying an ensign, indicating their nationality. Based on the illustrations, can you work out which part of a ship an ensign is traditionally flown from, and the nationalities of those four ships?

2. What do you think the Dutch word 'oost' means in English? It can be found prominently at the bottom of the map.

3. The image at the top-left-hand corner of the map is a representation of a prominent land-based route used at the time for transporting goods.

    a. What is the name of this route, which stretched from Asia to Europe and was in use for over two millennia?

    b. Which word, derived from the Persian *kārwān* and which now describes a habitable vehicle in modern English, is a general descriptive name given to the method of transportation shown in the image, where traders travelled in groups during the long overland journeys?

c. Which animal related to the llama is pictured travelling with the traders?

4. Which modern island country, only partially illustrated on this map, has been given a name here that translates as 'New Holland'? What year was it 'discovered', according to the map?

5. The island known as Tasmania is now named after the first European to sight it, Abel Tasman. When Tasman first saw it, however, he named the land after his benefactor. What do you think was the name of his sponsor, based on the depiction of the island on this map?

6. This chart is printed on vellum (treated calf skin). Why do think this material was used, given that paper would have been available at the time of printing?

7. Which island shown on the map is now divided between Malaysia, Brunei and Indonesia? Part of the island was under Dutch control in the nineteenth and twentieth centuries.

8. What is the former name of the island country of Sri Lanka, which appears on this map? The historical name can still be found in the names of some varieties of tea produced in and exported from the region.

Portion of a map by Pieter Goos, produced around 1666.

NORTH AMERICA – Herman Moll

The map on the following page details the routes of ships of European imperial powers across the Atlantic. It gives explanations of place name changes, the dates Europeans arrived in certain locations, and the names of the indigenous peoples living across North and Central America. The map also has two interesting additions on the left-hand side: an illustrated description of the process of cod fishing in Newfoundland (shown enlarged below), and a series of close-ups showing major ports and harbours in North America.

COD FISHING

The image on the left shows the landing, curing and drying of cod in Newfoundland. Can you match each of the descriptions of the cod fishing process given below, taken from the original map, with one of the labels, A–L, on the illustration?

- A Press to extract the Oyl from ye Cods Livers

- Another Cask to receive ye Oyl

- Casks to receive ye Water & Blood that comes from ye Livers

- Salt Boxes

- The Cleansing of ye Cod

- The Dressers of ye Fish

- The Habit of ye Fishermen

- The Line

- The Trough into which they throw ye Cod when Dressed

- The manner of Carrying ye Cod

- The manner of Drying ye Cod

- The manner of Fishing

A map of North America created by Herman Moll, in around 1712.

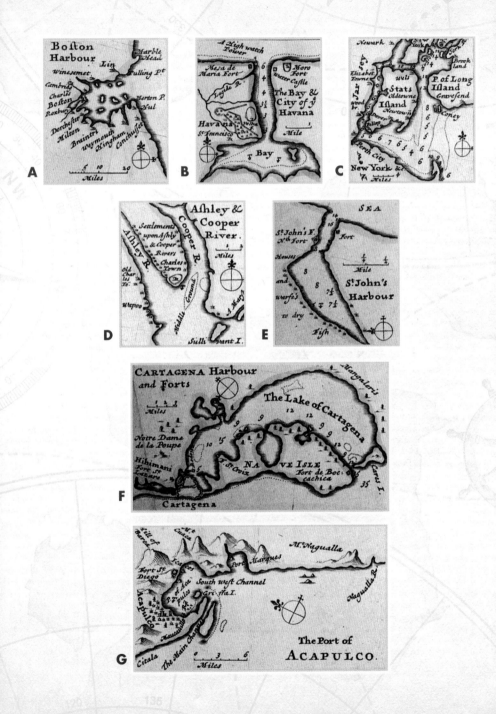

HARBOURS AND INLETS

The seven images shown opposite form the additional insets at the bottom-left of Herman Moll's map of North America. Can you match each of the statements below to one of these images?

1. This harbour was the site of a famous protest against the British Parliament, where a shipment of tea was thrown into the water

2. If you sailed into the north of this area today, you would come across a famous statue of a Roman goddess, partially built by Gustave Eiffel

3. This location can be found in an American state that has a 'north' equivalent

4. This harbour can be found on a Caribbean island now known for its socialist politics

5. This fortified city shares its name with a city in southern Spain

6. This harbour is on an island that gave its name to a large breed of dog

7. This port's official name includes a tribute to Benito Juárez, a former Mexican president

SOUTH AMERICA –
Johannes van Doetechum

Dating from around 1590, the map on the following pages provides
two different views of the southern part of South America.
The main map image is based on the explorations of Thomas
Cavendish, an English sea captain who was inspired by Francis
Drake to circumnavigate the world. The inset at the bottom-right,
reproduced below, was based on Spanish sources. On this map,
the letter ʃ corresponds to a modern 's'.

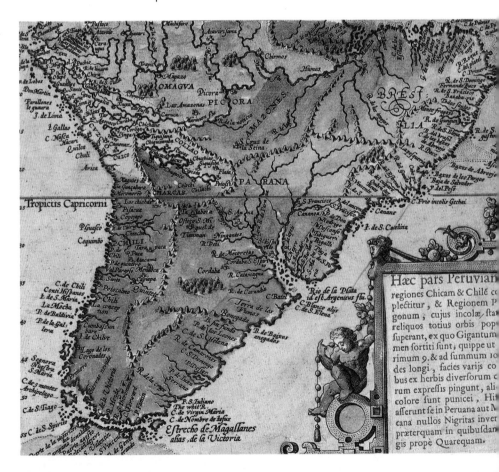

Use the full map and its inset, plus your general knowledge, to answer the following questions about South America and early European exploration of the area.

1. Why do you think the inset map shows more detail in the inland areas than the main map?

2. Ferdinand Magellan named a large region on the map after several fires he witnessed burning along the coast. Its modern name, 'Tierra del Fuego', is the Spanish for 'land of fire'.

    a. Can you find the old Spanish label for this region on the main map? It is very similar to the modern Spanish.

    b. In this region, can you find a smaller Portuguese name label that also translates as 'land of fires'? It can be found on the coastline, immediately west of a Latin place label that shares its name with an ill-fated Antarctic expedition led by Robert Falcon Scott.

    c. The area now known as Tierra del Fuego was later discovered to be an archipelago, albeit with one island substantially larger than the others. Why do you think it is represented as a large continental land mass on this map?

3. a. What is the modern English name for the navigable passage named in Latin on the main map as 'FRETUM MAGALANICUM', and in Spanish as *'Eſtrecho de Fernando Magallanes'*?

    b. Why do you think it is labelled twice, and in relatively large lettering?

Chart created by Joannes van Doetechum in 1590.

c. The smaller inset map gives, in Spanish, an additional former name for the passage, named for the first ship that passed through it. What do you think the name of the ship was?

4. Can you find a location that is directly north-east of an illustration of a forest, and shares its name (with the exception of one letter and excluding accents) with an Andalusian Spanish city?

5. a. Can you find a major river estuary whose name on the map translates as 'river of silver'? The name is written in Spanish, followed by a Latin explanation. It may be helpful to know that it is often referred to in English as the River Plate.

b. Which capital city can be found today on the southern bank of this estuary?

c. Which modern country is now located on the northern bank of the estuary?

6. Can you find, in the boxed text at the top right of the map, the Latin name of the well-known English sailor and explorer on whose voyages Thomas Cavendish based his explorations?

7. The sixth and seventh lines of the boxed text referred to in the previous question name, in Latin, an unusual 'fish' sighted by the explorers, which is now classified as a bird. Can you work out from the Latin text which animal is being discussed? This bird can still be found along the coast of South America.

8. The animal pictured in the centre of the mainland has a description that implies it can be found living 'on air'. Which animal native to South America do you think the image may represent?

9. The map gives three different scales for calculating distance, each with its own unit of measurement: 'Hiſpanicae leucæ', 'Miliaria Italica' and 'Miliaria Germanica', as shown here:

a. Which three European countries are represented in the names of the three units of distance?

b. What modern unit of distance does 'miliaria' refer to?

c. What archaic unit of distance do you think 'leucæ' refers to?

10. Which major lake on the border of modern Bolivia and Peru can be seen in this close-up of the inset map, below?

11. Which is the more northerly on the close-up in question 10 above: the historic capital of the Inca empire, or the location of the modern capital of Peru?

NORTH POLE – Gerard Mercator

The map on the following pages was created in 1595 by Gerard Mercator, the cartographer whose eponymous world map projection is still used for nautical charts. As well as his famous world map, Mercator produced maps of different parts of the world for an atlas. This sheet depicts the North Pole and the regions around it, in what is known as a polar projection.

Having never explored the North Pole himself, Mercator used information from various sources to construct his map, and what he compiled looks very different to how we understand the far north today.

Can you answer the following questions, which examine the curiosities shown on one of the first maps of the North Pole?

1. The archipelago of the Shetland Islands is depicted in the inset circle at the bottom-left-hand corner of the map.

    a. Where are these islands shown on the central map?

    b. Which Shetland island labelled on the inset close-up is also the name of one of the sea areas used in the modern-day shipping forecast? The map spelling does not exactly match the modern spelling.

    c. Which Scottish archipelago has been labelled 'Orcades', shown to the west of the Shetland Islands?

    d. Both of these archipelagos were pledged to Scotland just over a century before this map was made. Which country – also pictured on this map – had ruled over them until that point?

2. Which archipelago is represented in the inset circle at the top-right-hand corner of the map, labelled 'Farre insuľę'? 'Insuľę' is the Latin for 'islands'.

3. Before the first navigation of the Bering Strait, a legendary passage separating the Asian and North American continents would frequently appear on maps, despite there having been no confirmation of its existence. Can you find it on this map? The name label is not written in English, but part of the name is one letter away from the word 'Asian'.

4. The island in the top-left-hand corner close-up of the map is labelled 'Fri lant inſula', meaning 'Frisland Island'. The island and its smaller counterpart on the main map enjoy a high level of detail, with several named settlements and smaller outlying islands also illustrated. What is particularly unusual about the representation of Frisland as shown here, compared to modern maps?

5. Can you find an island erroneously added to this and other contemporary maps of the period, whose appearance may be the result of a misunderstanding of the spelling of nearby Greenland?

6. What kind of objects did some sixteenth-century scholars think were the reason that compasses point north? There are three labelled on the map.

7. The red circle labelled as the 'Circulus Arcticus', or Arctic Circle, is shown as intersecting mainland Iceland. On modern maps, does mainland Iceland sit entirely within or entirely outside the Arctic Circle?

Agama

Circulus

Obila flu.   Canaoga

Zubilaga   Obila flu.
                           Chiagiga

California regio
sola fama Hispanis
nota

Cogib. flu.

Lago de
Conibas

Hic mare est
dulcium aquarum,
cuius terminum ig‐
norari Canadenses
ex relatu Saguen‐
iensium aiunt

Oceanus 19 ostijs inter has in‐
sulas irrumpens 5 euripos fa‐
cit quibus indesinenter sub‐
septentrionem fertur, atq. ibi
in viscera terre absorbetur
Rupes que sub polo est ambit
circiter 33 leucarum habet

Gradus 75 latitudinis   80   85   90

Hæc insula optima
est et saluberrima
totius septen‐
trionis.

Hic eurpus 5 in‐
greditur ostijs
et quotannis ad
5 circiter menses
congelatus manet
latitudinem habet
37 leucarum.

Mare gla:

Groclant

Hit als Sandersons
Hope prom.

E. Cumberlands
Isles.

Fretum   Dau

GROENLAND

OCEANUS S

Regina Elizabe
thæ prom.

ISLAND

TRIONAL

Map of the
Northern
regions
by Gerard
Mercator.

ISLAND OF CALIFORNIA –
Hendrick Doncker

On many seventeenth-century maps California appears as a large island rather than as part of mainland North America. The map on the opposite page is a section of a map by Dutch publisher Hendrick Doncker, created in 1661. Use this map and your general knowledge to answer the following questions about the 'island' of California.

1. Explorers thought that California was an island after seeing the end of the long Californian peninsula. To which modern-day country does this peninsula belong?

2. a. What function do the decorative tendrils on the map serve?
b. And what do you notice about the orientation of the various lines of latitude marked on the map?
c. Based on your answer to question b), which is the odd map out?

3. Turn forward to the 'Fool's Cap' map of the world shown on page 266–7, which was published circa 1590. What do you notice about the way California is presented on that map relative to this one, given that this map was made later, in 1661?

4. Based on the names given to the regions of the mainland next to the 'island' of California, which European country do you think colonised this part of North America?

Opposite:
Chart by Hendrik Doncker, c.1661.

Pascaart
vertoonende de Zeecusten van
Chili, Peru, Hispania Nova, Nova Gra
nada, en California.
't Amsterdam.
By Hendrick Doncker Boeckverkooper in de
Nieuwe brugh steegh in 't Stuiermans gereedt-
schap.

5. a. Can you find the label for a group of Pacific islands (on one of the inset maps) that was given two competing names by Spanish explorers? The first part of the label translates to English as 'islands of the sails', and may refer to the sails on boats used by the Chamorro people who are indigenous to the area. The second part of the label shows the islands were also given an alternative name meaning 'thieves' in Spanish, which may stem from a clash between the Spanish and the Chamorro.

b. What is the modern name of these islands, shared with an ocean trench where the Challenger Deep can be found?

6. A close-up of the scale used on this map is shown below. What does this scale reveal about how cartographers from different countries drew their maps in this time period?

Duytsche mylen is in een graadt.

RAILWAY TIME

Until the Industrial Revolution brought railways and the need for a standardised timetable, the UK operated under a system of 'local mean time', where clocks in different towns and cities would show different times to London's local time. To mitigate confusion and prevent accidents on the tracks between towns, Great Western Railway brought in 'Railway Time', which was eventually implemented at all stations in 1847.

The map on the following page shows which public clocks in Great Britain still operated according to 'local time zones' in 1852. London is given as a time zone shift of 0, indicated by the bold line, operating on 'Greenwich Time'. The axis along the bottom of the map shows the time differences in minutes: east of the bold line is minutes fast, while west of the bold line is minutes slow. The key underneath the map's title indicates which town clocks showed Greenwich time, and which showed local time.

Given these facts, can you use the map to answer these questions about the time shown on different town clocks around Great Britain? Please note, cities not keeping Greenwich Time are indicated on the map in italics.

1. What is the greatest time difference between any two towns shown on this map?

2. What is the time difference between Berwick and Wolverhampton, according to the map?

3. If the time is 11.34 a.m. in Bristol, what time is it in Tonbridge, according to the map?

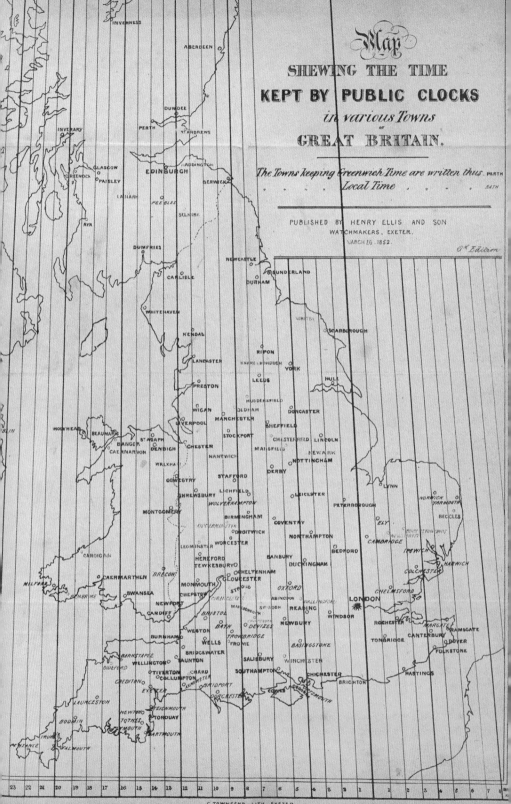

Map

SHEWING THE TIME

KEPT BY PUBLIC CLOCKS

in various Towns
or
GREAT BRITAIN.

The Towns keeping Greenwich Time are written thus . . PERTH
Local Time . . . . BATH

PUBLISHED BY HENRY ELLIS AND SON
WATCHMAKERS, EXETER.
MARCH 26. 1852.

6th Edition

4. How many English towns north of Leicester kept local time in 1852, according to the map?

5. Which university has the smaller time difference to St Andrew's: the University of Oxford or the University of Cambridge?

An artwork depicting the Meridian Line at the Royal Observatory in Greenwich, which forms the basis of the international time zone system and Greenwich Mean Time.

Left:
A map from the 1850s showing the different local times across the UK before standard time was introduced.

FOOL'S CAP WORLD MAP

The map on the following pages was made around the year 1580 by an unknown cartographer, although it borrows heavily from an earlier woodcut map made by Jean de Gourmont. As well as the projection of the world (based on the third 'Typus Orbis Terrarum' by Abraham Ortelius) and the illustration of the 'fool's cap', this document features multiple Latin inscriptions from different sources.

English translations of some of these Latin inscriptions have been encrypted below. Each quote has been encoded using a simple alphabet-shift cipher, in which each letter in the quote has been shifted forward by a fixed number of positions in the alphabet. Shifts past the end of the alphabet continue again from A. For example, NAVIGATE with each letter shifted forward by two would become PCXKICVG.

The correct shift numbers are provided along with the provenance of each quote to help you, although the lists are not given in the same order. Can you work out the size of each quote's shift, decode the quotes, and match them to the Latin quote on the illustration they were translated from? The location of each Latin quote on the illustration is labelled with the corresponding number of the encrypted quote below.

1. Pstb ymdxjqk

2. R khdg, zruwkb ri d grvh ri khooheruh

3. Dov kvlz uva ohcl kvurlf'z lhyz?

4. Vjg pwodgt qh hqqnu ku kphkpkvg

5. Ejwrch xo ejwrcrnb, juu rb ejwrch

6. SI, xli asvvmiw sj xli asvph; sl, Isa qygl xvmzmepmxc mw xlivi mr xli asvph

7. Kvv wox kbo gsdryed coxco

8. Grr znotmy gxk bgtoze, he kbkxe sgt robotm

- From Ecclesiastes 1:15 – shift: 2
- From an unknown source – shift: 3
- From the 'Satires' of Aulus Persius Flaccus – shift: 4
- From the Greek dictum 'gnothi seauton' reputedly inscribed on the temple of Apollo at Delphi – shift: 5
- From Psalm 39:6 – shift: 6
- Ascribed to Lucius Annaeus Cornutus, a Roman stoic philosopher from the first century AD – shift: 7
- From Ecclesiastes 1:2 – shift: 9
- From Jeremiah 10:14 – shift: 10

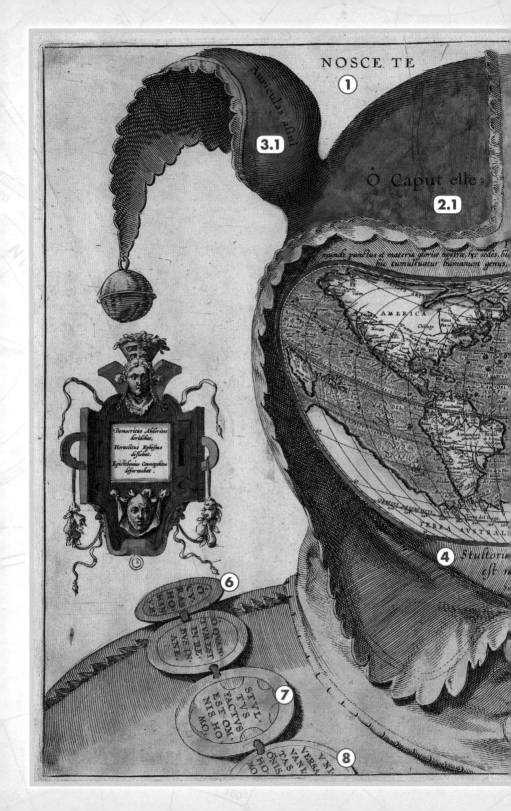

THE SPANISH ARMADA

The Armada Portrait of Queen Elizabeth I, 1533–1603, *one of the most iconic images of Elizabeth I ever produced.*

In 1588, Don Alonso Pérez de Guzmán, 7th Duke of Medina Sidonia, led a naval attack that aimed to overthrow Queen Elizabeth I. The Spanish Armada, as it was known, set out from Spain on 12 July towards the Netherlands, attempting to meet the Duke of Parma there before invading. Lord Howard of Effingham and Sir Francis Drake led the English ships, and the Spanish were eventually forced to retreat back to Spain by sailing up and around the coast of Scotland.

Robert Adams created a series of eleven maps illustrating the progress of the battle. Eight of them are pictured on the following pages. Can you match each event on the timeline shown here with the number of the map that illustrates the event? The timeline is not to scale.

29 July: The Spanish Armada near the Cornwall coast

30–31 July: The English pursue the Spanish along the coast of Cornwall towards Plymouth

31 July–1 August: The English fleet pursue the Armada near the Devonshire coast

4 August: The two sides battle near the Isle of Wight

4–6 August: The Spanish fleet are chased towards Calais, France

7 August: The English fleet launch a fireship attack against the Spanish near the French coast

8 August: The two sides battle near Gravelines on the French coast

The Spanish Armada sail around Britain and Ireland, following the path marked on this map to return to Spain

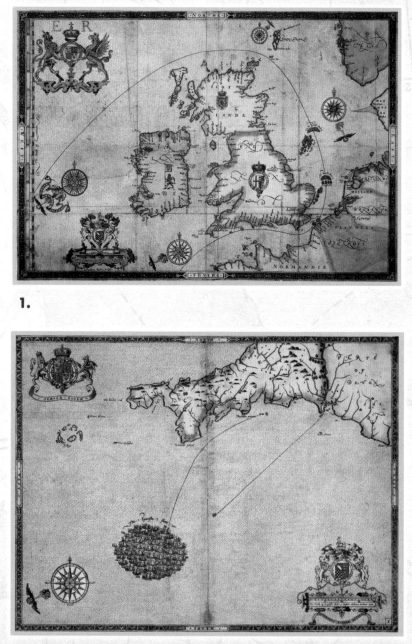

1.

2.

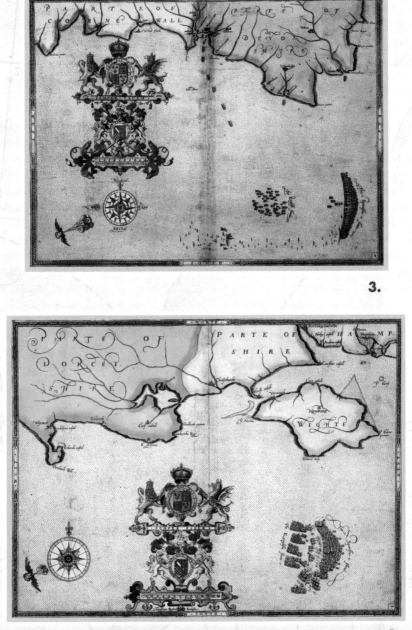

3.

4.

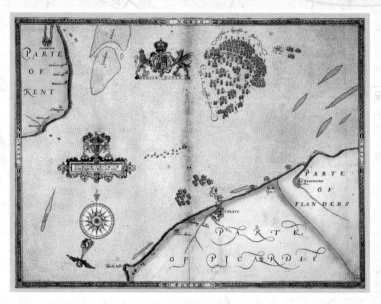

5.

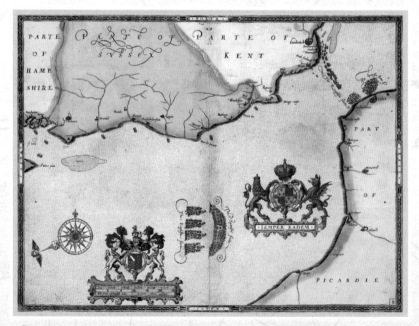

6.

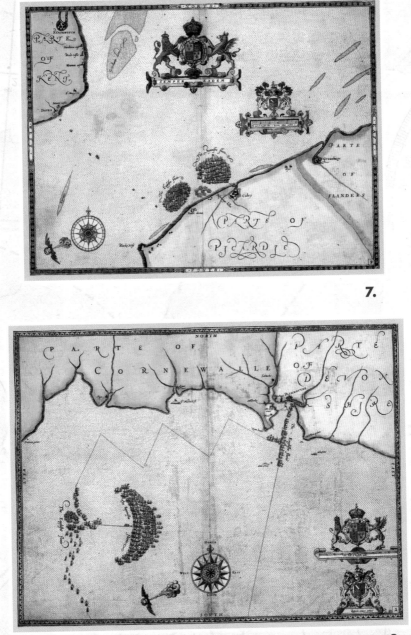

7.

8.

SOLUTIONS

Compass Variation – Edmond Halley

1. a. The dedication reads, 'To his Royal Highness Prince GEORGE of DENMARK, LORD HIGH ADMIRALL (*sic*) of ENGLAND'. Prince George was Queen Anne's husband.

b. Prince George became the ceremonial head of the Royal Navy in 1702, as revealed by the title 'Lord High Admirall' (*sic*).

2. a. Astronomy – Edmond Halley became Astronomer Royal in 1720.

b. Halley's Comet, which is visible to the naked eye every 75–76 years.

3. a. Madagascar. The island was previously named St Laurence, after the Roman martyr.

b. Three. The bold line at the northern end of the island shows 20 degrees of west variation, and the two dotted lines beneath it show 21 and 22 degrees of west variation.

4. 5 degrees of variation east. This isogonic line is furthest to the right on the map, and passes through Yedso at the top of the map, in the location of the Kamchatka peninsula. Then, further south, it passes through an area joining Hollandia Nova (Australia) and Terra de Papos Novaguinea (roughly equivalent to the island of New Guinea, which today includes the countries of Papua New Guinea and Indonesia).

5. Russia, labelled as 'Russia or Muscovy' on the map. Muscovy was a medieval principality centred around the city of Moscow, which formed the core of the modern country.

6. The Adriatic Sea is labelled as 'GULF OF VENICE'.

7. a. Côte d'Ivoire, or Ivory Coast.

b. Five degrees of west variation, indicated by the bold dotted line south of the 'Gold Coast' label.

c. Ivory. Both areas are named after the main products that were found there: elephant ivory tusks and gold were key exports from these areas.

8. Monte Negro, labelled in the approximate area of Angola in south-west Africa. The name lives on to some extent, since Epupa Falls (not marked on the map), found on the border of Namibia and Angola, is now known as Monte Negro Falls to Angolans.

World Map – Pierre Du Val

1. a. The label 'Ligne du Premier Meridien' is highlighted in red, and intersected by the horizontal lines indicating the 50th and 60th degrees north of latitude.

  b. Iceland, labelled 'Islande' on the map. The Arctic Circle is labelled (at the top left) as 'Cercle du Pole Arctique'.

  c. The 20-degree line of longitude on this map is in roughly the same location as the modern prime meridian, running through the UK, France, Spain and western Africa.

2. a. The Azores. They are labelled as 'I. Açores' on the map, a name which derives from the Portuguese word for the Northern goshawk (which is ironically not actually found on the islands).

  b. The Grand Banks of Newfoundland, east of Canada, are labelled on the map as 'le Grand Banc'. Marked by an area of dots, they indicate relatively shallow waters in the north Atlantic.

3. The island of Bermuda, labelled 'I. Bermudes' on this map, can be found between the 310th and 320th lines of longitude. The Bermuda Triangle is the infamous area to which it lends its name, roughly bounded by Bermuda, Puerto Rico and Florida.

4. a. The 20th north line of latitude. The ship is to the bottom-right of the label 'MER DE NORT'.

  b. Saint Helen, labelled as 'I. Ste Helene'. The abbreviation 'Ste' indicates a female saint in French.

  c. Tristan de Cunha, labelled 'I. Tristan de Cunha' on this map.

World Map – Pierre Hamon

1. North is drawn at the bottom of the map, and south at the top, meaning the continents have the appearance of being upside-down relative to most map projections.

2. a. The labels 'MER AVSTRALE' and 'LA MER DV SV' both translate from French as 'southern sea' (or 'sea of the south' for the latter, more precisely). Australia is named from the Latin, 'Australis', meaning 'southern'.

    b. The label 'MER AVSTRALE' indicates the modern Southern (or Antarctic) Ocean, and the label 'LA MER DV SV' indicates the modern Pacific Ocean.

3. a. North. The use of 'septentrional' to mean 'north' or 'northerly' comes from the Latin name for the constellations of Ursa Major and Ursa Minor (literally 'seven plough-oxen'), which is visible in the northern hemisphere.

    b. The label 'MER SEPTENTRIONALE' can be found at the bottom of the map, in the approximate area of the Arctic Ocean.

4. Java, as seen in the label 'Iava la Grande', where the 'I' should be read as a 'J'. Since 'Grande' is the French word for 'large', the label 'Iava la Grande' helps indicate the large size of the island, fitting with Marco Polo's claim.

5. a. 'REGION INCONGNEVE'. This can be found twice near the bottom of the map, on the continents of Asia and North America.

    b. 'BARBARIE' – this label can be found on the north coast of Africa.

    c. The label 'MER DE FRANCE', towards the bottom-right corner of the map, matches the mapmaker Pierre Hamon's French nationality. This area of ocean spans the stretch between France and (modern-day) Canada. Canada itself is labelled on the map as 'LA NOUVELLE FRANCE occidentalle', i.e., 'western new France'.

6. The island 'Isle des Geantz' translates as 'Island of Giants' – a place that sounds like it might be a location in the 1726 book *Gulliver's Travels*. It can be found to the top left of the map.

7. The Black Sea.

8. The Nile.

9. Greenland is shown as being a peninsula attached to mainland Europe on the map. As well as being an island, the real Greenland is much further west (closer to modern-day Canada) than pictured here.

East Indies – Pieter Goos

1. An ensign is traditionally flown at the stern (back) of a ship. The ensigns on all four ships are Dutch flags, reflecting the nationality of the mapmaker.

2. 'Oost', as in the large caption 'OOST INDIEN', is the Dutch word for 'east'. The majority of the area shown on the map was known as the East Indies, contrasting with the West Indies.

3. a. The Silk Road.
   b. Caravan.
   c. Camels.

4. Australia, in 1644. The label reads 'Hollandia Nova: Detecta A° 1644', with the second part meaning 'detected in the year 1644'.

5. Anthony van Diemen. The incomplete outline at the bottom right of the map – representing modern Tasmania – bears the label 'Anthoni van Diemens Landt'.

6. Vellum was more robust – and more waterproof – than paper, which made it a preferable material for maritime navigators.

7. Borneo.

8. Ceylon.

North America – Herman Moll
Cod Fishing

A. The Habit of ye Fishermen

B. The Line

C. The manner of Fishing

D. The Dressers of ye Fish

E. The Trough into which they throw ye Cod when Dressed

F. Salt Boxes

G. The manner of Carrying ye Cod

H. The Cleansing of ye Cod

I. A Press to extract ye Oyl from ye Cods Livers

J. Casks to receive ye Water & Blood that comes from ye Livers

K. Another Cask to receive the Oyl

L. The manner of Drying ye Cod

Harbours and Inlets

1. A. Boston Harbour is the site of the Boston Tea Party, a key protest in the build-up to the American Revolution.

2. C. The famous statue is the Statue of Liberty, located in New York Harbour.

3. D. The Ashley and Cooper rivers can be found in South Carolina, which borders North Carolina.

4. B. Havana is the capital of Cuba, which is led by the Communist Party of Cuba.

5. F. Cartagena, Colombia shares its name with the city of Cartagena in Murcia, southern Spain.

6. E. St John's Harbour is located on the Canadian island of Newfoundland, where Newfoundland dogs were bred as working dogs.

7. G. Acapulco's full, modern-day name is Acapulco de Juárez.

South America – Johannes van Doetiechum

1. The inset map was created using Spanish sources, who are likely to have had a more in-depth knowledge of the geography of the land following Spain's conquests and occupation of South American regions.

2. **a.** Terra del Fugo, labelled at the bottom of the map.

   b. The label 'Terra do Fogos' can be found just west of the label 'Terra Nova', both on the western side of the Terra del Fugo region shown.

   c. It was once believed that a large undiscovered continent must cover the southern half of the planet in order to 'balance' the northern continental land masses already discovered. The hypothetical continent was often referred to as 'Terra Australis', meaning 'Southern Land'. It would not be correct to say it was based on any sightings or narratives of Antarctica, since this was not recorded by explorers until the nineteenth century.

3. **a.** The Strait of Magellan.

   b. When it was discovered, the Strait was believed to be the only passage between the Atlantic and Pacific oceans, and therefore the only passage able to facilitate a circumnavigation of the world. This would have been enormously significant to navigators and cartographers.

   c. Victoria. The inscription on the inset map reads 'Eſtrecho de Magallanes alias de la Victoria'.

4. Cordaba – this location is now known as Córdoba. It can be found just to the right of the large image of an animal towards the centre of the map.

5. **a.** Rio de la Plata. It can be found on the east coast of South America.

   b. Buenos Aires.

   c. Uruguay.

6. 'Franciſcus Draco' – the Latin name for Francis Drake – can be found in the fifth line of the text.

7. Penguins. The text refers to an 'Inſulam Penguinorum', which translates as 'Penguin Island'.

8. A sloth. The quality of living 'on air' derives from the view of a couple of European natural historians in the sixteenth century, who suggested that sloths lived on air because no one saw them eating.

9. a. Spain ('Hiſpanicae' meaning Spanish), Italy ('Italica' meaning Italian) and Germany ('Germanica' meaning German).

   b. Miles.

   c. Leagues.

10. Lake Titicaca, shown as 'Titicacha lacus' to the right of the close-up.

11. Lima, Peru's capital city, can be found in the top-left corner, and is the more northerly. Cuzco (or Cusco) is the historic Inca capital and can be found in the centre of the map. The surrounding region is also labelled 'CVZCO'.

North Pole – Gerard Mercator

1. a. The Shetland Islands are at the very bottom centre of the main map.

   b. Fair Isle. Labelled 'Faire Il' on the close-up, this island gives its name to the sea area that surrounds it. It can also be seen on the main map, though its label is obscured by damage to the paper.

   c. Orkney.

   d. Norway.

2. The Faroe Islands. They can also be found on the main map, west of the Shetland Islands.

3. The Strait of Anian – labelled on this map as 'El streto de Anian' – can be found at the top of the map, near the red line representing the border of the Arctic Circle.

4. Frisland and its outlying islands are fictional. It is a phantom
   island that appeared on many maps for a further century after
   this map was created.
5. Groclant, north-west of the island of Greenland (labelled on
   this map as Groenland). It is thought that variation in the
   spelling of the real island of Greenland led cartographers to
   believe in the existence of two separate islands, located near
   one another, with similar names.
6. Large magnetic rocks. One can be seen in the middle of the
   map by the label 'POLVS ARCTICVS', with two others shown in
   the ocean above and to the right of it. Scientists believed that
   the variation in compass readings was caused by the presence
   of multiple magnetic rocks in the polar region.
7. Mainland Iceland is completely outside the modern Arctic
   Circle, although the Icelandic island of Grímsey, shown on this
   map as Grims ey, is intersected by it.

Island of California – Hendrick Doncker

1. Mexico.
2. **a.** The tendrils divide the map into four separate, non-
   continuous sections.
   b. As can be seen from the marking of the tropics of Cancer
   (*Tropicus Cancri*) and Capricorn (*Tropicus Capricorni*), and
   the equator (*Linia Aequinoctialis*), the orientation varies
   between the main map and the inset maps.
   c. The main map, since it is oriented so north faces to the left;
   the three inset maps have north to the top of the page.
3. The Fool's Cap map of the world shows California attached to
   the mainland, unlike this later map, making the Fool's Cap map
   more geographically accurate despite its earlier provenance.
   The persistent representation of California as an island is
   considered to be the result of cartographers replicating other

maps in lieu of using their own navigational experience, so mistakes were readily propagated.

4. Spain. Clues can be seen in the name Hispania, the Latin for 'Spain', which can be found in the label 'HISPANIA NOVA' towards the right-hand edge of the map. Granada, which can be found in the label 'NOVA GRANADA', is also a city located in southern Spain.

5. a. The label can be found towards the top-left corner of the map. 'Iſlas de las Velas' means 'islands of the sails', while 'Ladrones' is Spanish for 'thieves'. You can see both on this close-up:

b. The Mariana Islands. These share their name with the Mariana Trench, where Challenger Deep (the deepest point in the world's ocean) is located.

6. The scale is labelled 'Duytſche mylen', or 'Dutch miles', indicating that miles were not standardised at this point in history, and that the distance of a mile varied from country to country.

Railway Time

1. Yarmouth, at 6 minutes fast, and Penzance, at 22 minutes slow, give the greatest time difference on the map, at 28 minutes.

2. According to the map Berwick keeps Greenwich Time and Wolverhampton keeps local time, making the time difference 9 minutes.

3. 11.45 a.m. Tonbridge is shown as keeping Greenwich time, giving a time difference of 11 minutes.

4. None, according to this map.

5. Cambridge. Despite both Oxford and St Andrews being situated east of the Greenwich Time line, St Andrews keeps Greenwich Time, meaning Cambridge clocks are only one minute faster.

Fool's Cap World Map

1. Know thyself – shift 5, from the Greek dictum 'gnothi seauton' reputedly inscribed on the temple of Apollo at Delphi. This quote, 'Nosce te ipsum' in Latin, can be found above the cap.

2. O head, worthy of a dose of hellebore – shift 3, unknown source. This quote, 'Ô caput elleboro dignum' in Latin, can be found across the cap's brow.

3. Who does not have donkey's ears? – shift 7, ascribed to Lucius Annaeus Cornutus, a Roman stoic philosopher from the first century AD. This quote, 'Auriculas asini quis non habet' in Latin, can be found on the cap's ears.

4. The number of fools is infinite – shift 2, from Ecclesiastes 1:15. This quote, 'Stultorum infinitus est numerus' in Latin, can be found below the map.

5. Vanity of vanities, all is vanity – shift 9, from Ecclesiastes 1:2. This quote, 'Vanitas vanitatum et omnia vanitas' in Latin, can be found at the top of the jester's staff.

6. Oh, the worries of the world; oh, how much triviality is there in the world – shift 4, from the 'Satires' of Aulus Persius Flaccus. This quote, 'Ô curas hominum, Ô quantum est in rebus inane' in Latin, can be found on one of the discs on the jester's shoulder.

7. All men are without sense – shift 10, from Jeremiah 10:14. This quote, 'Stultus factus est omnis homo' in Latin, can be found on one of the discs on the jester's shoulder.

8. All things are vanity, by every man living – shift 6, from Psalm 39:6. This quote, 'Universa vanitas omnis homo' in Latin, can be found on one of the discs on the jester's shoulder.

The Spanish Armada

Timeline event	Map number
29 July: The Spanish Armada near the Cornwall coast	2
30–31 July: The English pursue the Spanish along the coast of Cornwall towards Plymouth	8
31 July–1 August: The English fleet pursue the Armada near the Devonshire coast	3
4 August: The two sides battle near the Isle of Wight	4
4–6 August: The Spanish fleet are chased towards Calais, France	6
7 August: The English fleet launch a fireship attack against the Spanish near the French coast	7
8 August: The two sides battle near Gravelines on the French coast	5
The Spanish Armada sail around Britain and Ireland, following a path marked on this map to return to Spain	1

NOTES

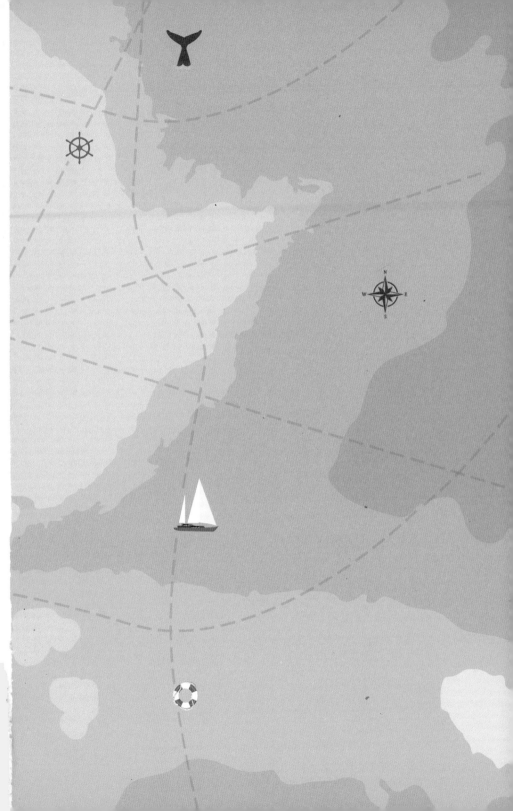

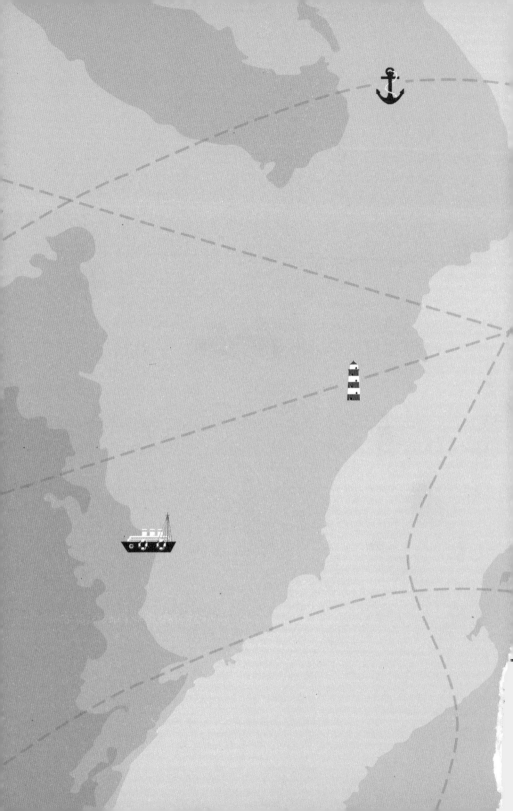